LOCOMOTION PAPERS | LP242

The Midland Railway route from Wolverhampton

The story of the line from Wolverhampton to Walsall, Sutton Park and Water Orton

by
Bob Yate

THE OAKWOOD PRESS

© Oakwood Press & Bob Yate 2018

Published by Oakwood Press, an imprint of Stenlake Publishing Ltd, 2018

British Library Cataloguing in Publication Data
A Record for this book is available from the British Library
ISBN 978 0 85361 449 4

Printed by Claro Print, Unit 2, Kirkhill House, 81 Broom Road East, Glasgow, G77 5LL

All rights reserved. No part of this book may be reproduced or transmitted in any form or by any means, electronic or mechanical, including photocopying, recording or by any information storage and retrieval system, without permission from the Publisher in writing.

Title page: Bowen-Cooke '7F' class 0-8-0 No. 49407 at North Walsall Junction with a coal train from the WWMJR direct line, probably destined for Birchills power station, around 1960. This locomotive was one of several fitted with a tender cab, most necessary when working tender-first across the Cannock Chase line in the depths of winter.
R. Selvey Collection

Front cover: A former LNWR '7F' class, unfortunately not identified, this time with a coal train heading west near Bentley around 1963, probably bound for the Wolverhampton goods yard. The engine seems to have only recently been applied with the yellow diagonal stripe on the cabside, indicating that it was not permitted to work beneath the overhead electric catenary.
R. Selvey Collection

Rear cover: Watching passing trains seems to have been a timeless pursuit, as evidenced by this small girl enjoying the progress of a Fowler '4F' 0-6-0 as it trundles along the Brownhills branch towards Aldridge during the last week of regular goods traffic in 1960. The location is the 'Rabbit Bridge' on Vigo Road, looking northwards.
Bill Mayo Collection

Oakwood Press, 54-58 Mill Square, Catrine, KA5 6RD,
Tel: 01290 551122 *Website:* www.stenlake.co.uk

Contents

	Introduction	5
Chapter One	**The Wolverhampton & Walsall Railway**	
	Formation of the company – Planning the route –	
	Construction of the line – Opening – Working the line	
	from 1872 to 1879	6
Chapter Two	**The Wolverhampton Walsall & Midland Junction Railway**	
	Formation of the company – Planning the route –	
	Construction of the line – Opening............................	17
Chapter Three	**Midland Railway improvements and expansion**	
	Major construction projects : Wolverhampton passenger	
	station, Wolverhampton goods depot, Wolverhampton Canal	
	goods depot, Walsall goods depots, Walsall engine shed	25
Chapter Four	**Other railways**	
	Unsuccessful lines that would have been linked: Walsall &	
	Wolverhampton Railway Extension, Wolverhampton &	
	Walsall Railway Bentley Branches, Wednesfield & Wyrley	
	Bank Railway, Essington & Ashmore Light Railway	39
Chapter Five	**Description of the line**	
	A journey from Wolverhampton via Walsall to Water Orton	
	detailing the stations, track layouts, items of operating interest	
	and other lineside features	45
Chapter Six	**Working the line, 1879-1965**	
	Details of MR, LMS and BR passenger, goods services and	
	trip workings in this period, locomotives and rolling stock	
	in use on the line, 'The Pines Express', GWR goods services,	
	excursions and special workings	85
Chapter Seven	**Closure and retrenchment**	
	Changes in status for the line, during the staggered closure	
	of the western half of the line.......................................	123
Chapter Eight	**The Brownhills branch**	
	Construction and opening of the Walsall Wood branch, and	
	the Walsall Wood extension to Cannock Chase, description of	
	the line, passenger and goods services, and the final closure	133
Chapter Nine	**Recent times**	
	A description of what remains of the original line today	155
Appendix One	**Industrial locomotives**	162
Appendix Two	**Local trip workings, June 1959 and June 1962**	168
	Chronology	171
	Bibliography and Acknowledgements	173
	Index...	175

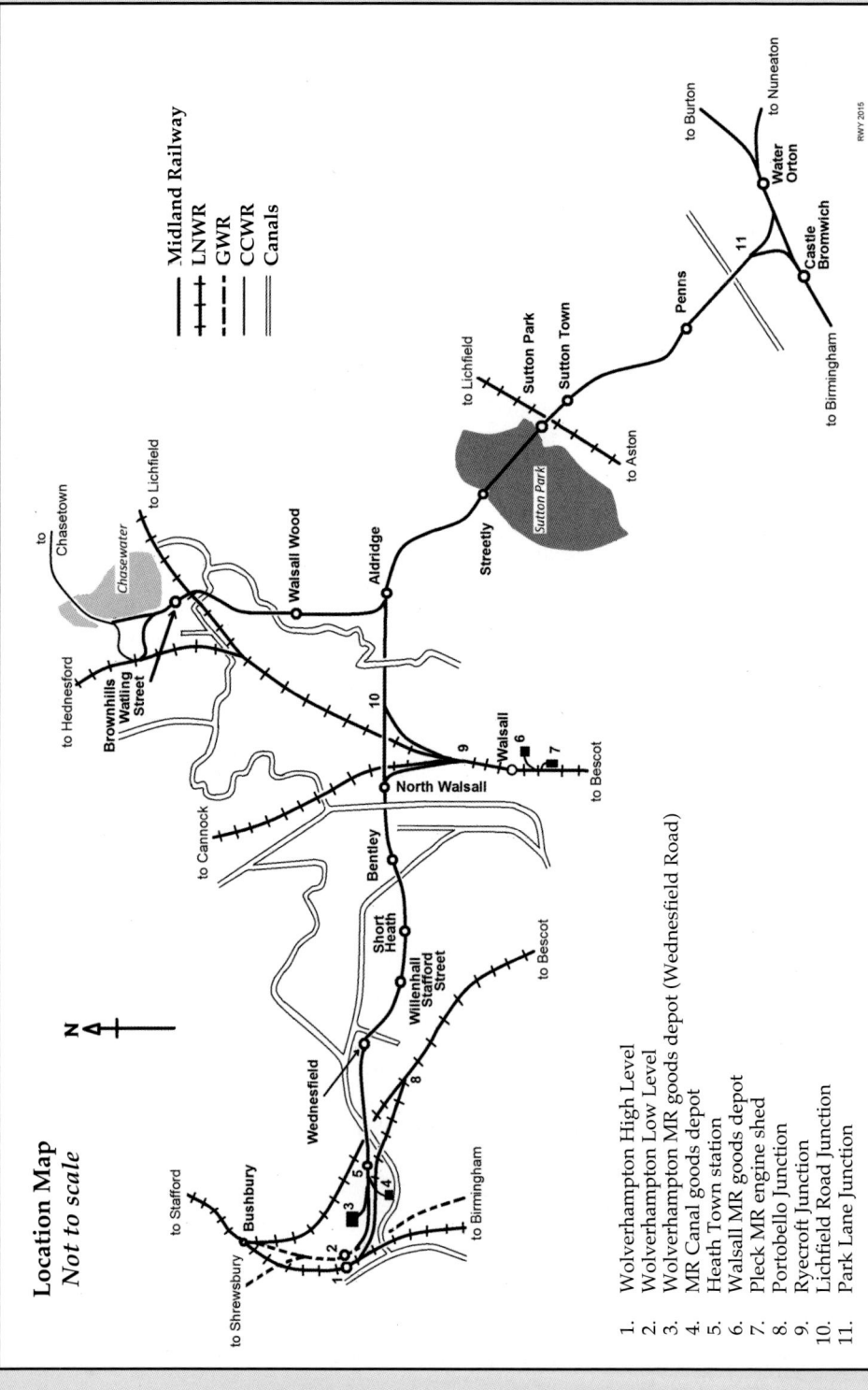

Introduction

The line was built in two separate parts. The Wolverhampton & Walsall Railway was first, being built by a nominally independent company, and was initially operated from 1872 by the LNWR with the MR having running powers. The LNWR acquired the company in 1875, but relinquished ownership to the MR the following year. The second section was built by the MR from Walsall to Water Orton, opening in 1879. Even though this included a triangular junction at Walsall, there was never a great deal of through traffic directly between the two sections. Most services ran into Walsall, some reversing before continuing their journeys.

Competition between the MR on the first line and the LNWR on its two alternative routes between Wolverhampton and Walsall was fierce until a traffic sharing agreement was introduced in 1909. Thereafter, services and routes were shared until this line lost its passenger service in 1930, and so became one of those freight-only routes rarely visited (and for the most part, rarely photographed) over the years. Ultimately, the building of the M6 motorway in 1964 severed the line at Bentley, near Walsall. The line was cut back in stages, with the goods yard at Wolverhampton not finally succumbing until 1990.

On the eastern section the passenger service from Walsall to Birmingham via Sutton Park thrived, until the advent of personal transport in the 1960s seriously affected traffic levels and the passenger service was withdrawn in 1965. Nonetheless, the route proved to be a convenient link for freight traffic from the north-west to the south-west avoiding the busiest routes through Birmingham, and usefully linking the marshalling yards at Bescot (LNWR) and Washwood Heath (MR). These same functions are still performed today, and much local pressure is being brought to restore passenger services to the line, which is maintained to passenger standards.

The route spawned one branch line, running from Aldridge to Brownhills which first opened in 1882. Although the passenger service here was another early casualty, finishing in 1930, several collieries, brickworks and other businesses in the area continued to be served until closure of the truncated remaining section in 1969.

The promotion, construction and opening of each of these lines are given in detail. The effect of local and national events on these lines, and the changing relationship with other lines in this congested West Midlands area are also examined. Traffic levels, locomotive workings, and special events on each of the sections are covered in detail, along with the connecting industrial lines.

The following abbreviations are used throughout the text:

BCN	Birmingham Canal Navigation
BR	British Railways ; British Rail
BW&SVR	Birmingham, Wolverhampton & Stour Valley Railway
CCWR	Cannock Chase & Wolverhampton Railway
dmu	Diesel multiple unit
GJR	Grand Junction Railway
GWR	Great Western Railway
LMR	London Midland Region of British Railways
LMSR	London Midland & Scottish Railway
LNWR	London & North Western Railway
MR	Midland Railway
P&WR	Portobello & Wolverhampton Railway
S&BR	Shrewsbury & Birmingham Railway
SSR	South Staffordshire Railway
WR	Western Region of British Railways
WWMJR	Wolverhampton Walsall & Midland Junction Railway
WWR	Wolverhampton & Walsall Railway

'Up' trains are those running eastwards from Wolverhampton to Walsall and Water Orton. 'Down' trains run in the opposite direction.

Chapter One

The Wolverhampton & Walsall Railway

Formation and planning

The first scheme to link Wolverhampton and Walsall was that of the Portobello and Wolverhampton Railway (P&WR), whose Act (Vict. 10 and 11, cap. 188) was passed by Parliament on 9th July, 1847. This line was supported by the London & North Western Railway (LNWR), and was to run from the Grand Junction (GJR) line at Portobello to join the Birmingham, Wolverhampton & Stour Valley Railway (BW&SVR) then just beginning construction, in the centre of Wolverhampton. At that time, the nearest that the LNWR came to Wolverhampton was the former GJR station at Wednesfield Heath, over a mile from the town centre. The primary intention of the P&WR was to give the LNWR access to a station in the heart of this town, and not as a means of linking the two towns. Walsall passengers would have had to use the LNWR station at Bescot, accessed by a horse omnibus from the centre of Walsall. The LNWR involvement is clear in that section 30 of the Act gave the P&WR power to sell the line to the LNWR or to agree working with the LNWR, and section 31 for the line to be constructed jointly with the LNWR, or leased to the LNWR.

However, the BW&SVR line included a connection from the GJR at Bushbury to a new 'General' (later High Level) Station in Wolverhampton, before continuing to its new station in Birmingham (to become 'New Street'). Thus, traffic to and from the north into Wolverhampton and Birmingham would have a more direct line, and the centre of Wolverhampton would also be served. The LNWR had taken a lease of the BW&SVR in late 1846, and so by the following year when this Act was passed, the Portobello line was seen as unnecessary. Thus the powers in the P&WR Act were allowed to lapse, and the line was not built at this time, although as we shall see, it was eventually constructed under entirely different powers in 1881.

Nevertheless, there was a local need for a direct connection between the two towns. Whilst Walsall had developed considerable metal working industries and had become rightly proud of its leather working businesses, Wolverhampton had developed further so that it became the 'elder brother' of the two towns. Walsall folk preferred to visit Wolverhampton rather than Birmingham for their shopping and to consult the professional services located there, and only partly because it was nearer. In addition, by the 1860s Walsall still did not have direct access to the main line services, and so to travel any distance the inhabitants had to go via Birmingham New Street. This was particularly annoying if they wished to travel to the North-West or to North Wales, as their journey commenced in the opposite direction (although a more direct, but somewhat slower route existed via Rugeley and Stafford). So it was at this time that a group of local businessmen began to promote the Wolverhampton & Walsall Railway (WWR). This was at the time of the 'Second Railway Mania' and drew attention from other interested investors.

Plans were deposited at Stafford County Court at 3.25 pm on 30th November, 1864 for the line, which was stated to be of 6 miles 36 chains and 66 links (just under 6½ miles). At Wolverhampton there were to be junctions with the LNWR near to High Level station and to the Great Western Railway (GWR) at their Low Level station. This latter line would branch from the WWR main running line and was of 39 chains (½ mile) length at a ruling gradient of 1 in 100, which was also given as the ruling gradient for the remainder of the line. Intermediate stations were planned at Wednesfield Heath (just west of the crossing over the GJR line and the Wyrley and Essington Canal), Wednesfield (on the Wednesfield to Portobello road), Willenhall (on Wednesfield Road), Short Heath (at Bentley, on the Walsall to Bentley road) and North Walsall (at Rushall, on the Bloxwich to Walsall road). The line was to enter Walsall from the north, joining the South Staffordshire Railway (SSR) at Ryecroft Junction.

The company obtained an Act of Parliament (Vict. 28 and 29, cap. 181) which was enacted on 29th June, 1865, incorporating the company and requiring construction within five years. However, the route was changed, as the line connecting to the LNWR at Wolverhampton was omitted; instead, the only connection at Wolverhampton was described as a junction 'with the GWR at 140 yards from north-west end of tunnel mouth abutting on Messrs Sparrows' Iron Works'. The route into Walsall also changed, now approaching from the south, crossing Long Street and 'to Walsall at south side of Park Street and Wolverhampton Road at 60 yards on west side of centre of south parapet of Park Street bridge over South Staffordshire Railway'. In other words, the proposal was to build a new station on the west side of the existing LNWR station (opened by the SSR in 1849). This would have required the line, as it approached the Bentley area, to take a 90 degree turn to the south, followed by another similar turn to the east, then to the north, and either a separate running line in from the south, or running powers over the LNWR South Staffordshire Railway. This Act also enabled the LNWR to contribute to the cost of construction.

Shortly after the Act was passed, the company issued its Prospectus. This listed the Chairman as being the Earl of Lichfield, the Deputy Chairman as Edwin Dixon of Wolverhampton and 12 Directors. Of these, 10 were local persons, with the remaining two from London. Edwin Dixon lived at Cleveland House, Cleveland Street, Wolverhampton and was the owner of a wrought iron tube works. The most interesting person here is Ralph Anstruther Earle, of Park Street, Grosvenor Square, London who was a member of the prominent Earle family of Liverpool. Born in 1835, he became a member of the British Embassy in Paris in 1854, and in 1856 he met Disraeli who was visiting there and the two formed something of a bond. Shortly after, he started to supply Disraeli with detailed and sensitive diplomatic information which was useful to Disraeli's political ambitions. Disraeli became his mentor, and with his help Dixon was elected as MP for Berwick in 1859, but resigned the same year to take on the position as secretary to Disraeli. He continued to provide Disraeli with useful political information, from a variety of sources, and in 1865 was elected as MP for Maldon, Essex. Relations between the two seemed to have cooled during 1866-67, and after Disraeli's first, short period as Prime Minister in 1868, Dixon

WOLVERHAMPTON & WALSALL RAILWAY COMPANY.

INCORPORATED BY 28 & 29 VICTORIA CAP. 181.

CAPITAL £120,000 IN 12,000 SHARES OF £10 EACH.

Deposit £1 per Share on Application and £1 per Share on Allotment.

Chairman.
THE RIGHT HON. THE EARL OF LICHFIELD.

Deputy Chairman.
EDWIN DIXON, Esq., Wolverhampton.

Directors.
THOMAS BARKER, Esq., The Birches, near Codsall
WILLIAM DEAKIN, Esq., Willenhall.
EDWARD JOHN GIBBS, Esq., Wolverhampton
RALPH ANSTRUTHER EARLE, Esq., Park Street, Grosvenor Square, London
MOSES IRONMONGER, Esq., Wolverhampton
SAMUEL LOVERIDGE, Esq., Chapel Ash, Wolverhampton
RICHARD NUGENT, Esq., Ebury Street, London
FREDERICK CHARLES PERRY, Esq., Dunston, near Stafford
JAMES TILDESLEY, Esq., Willenhall
GEORGE LEES UNDERHILL, Esq., Wolverhampton
BENJAMIN URWICK, Esq., Willenhall
FREDERICK WALTON, Esq., Wolverhampton

Engineer.
JOHN ADDISON, Esq.

Solicitors.
Messrs. BAXTER, ROSE, NORTON, & Co., London.
Messrs. H. & J. F. UNDERHILL, } Wolverhampton.
Messrs. CORSER & FOWLER,

Bankers.
THE BILSTON DISTRICT BANKING COMPANY, Wolverhampton.
London Agents, Messrs. GLYN & CO.
THE MIDLAND BANKING COMPANY, (Limited) Wolverhampton.
London Agents, LONDON & COUNTY BANK.

Brokers.
Mr. JOHN UNDERHILL, Wolverhampton.
Mr. J. SMITH, 28, Bennett's Hill, Birmingham.
Mr. W. HARTRIDGE, 80, Old Broad Street, London.

This Company has obtained an Act of Parliament for the construction of a Railway between two of the principal towns in Staffordshire, Wolverhampton and Walsall. The proposed Railway is also intended to afford accomodation to the populous districts of Wednesfield Heath, Wednesfield, Willenhall, and Bentley, and to develope a large Mineral District, considerable portions of which possess no Railway accomodation.

There are upwards of 100 miles of Railway in the district of South Staffordshire known as "the Black Country," carrying daily an enormous and rapidly increasing passenger and goods traffic. The existing railways however do not supply the important towns of Wolverhampton, Willenhall, and Walsall, with that direct communication which is imperatively required, and the want of which has been long felt.

did not contest his Maldon seat in 1869. Thereafter, he concentrated on a financial career, during which he successfully negotiated a railway building contract in Turkey in 1869 for Baron Hirsch for which he earned himself some £10,000. He died 10 years later at the early age of 45. So there is evidence of his interest in railway construction and finance. Furthermore, he was related to Sir Hardman Earle, who was one of the Directors of the Grand Junction Railway and later, the London & North Western Railway - so given his fondness for intrigue, there is a possibility that in 1865 Ralph was representing the LNWR on the Board of the WWR.

The WWR Prospectus made much of the shortness of the route between the two towns (6½ miles), as compared to the three existing LNWR alternative routes of 9¾, 10 and 11 miles. The industry of the area was not forgotten, and the company had already made an agreement with the LNWR to work the railway and to exclusively carry all traffic between the two towns on the WWR. Also recorded was the appointment of John Addison as Engineer for the line.

2

The present circuitous route between Wolverhampton and Walsall is either by Bushbury Junction, down the old Grand Junction Line to Bescot Junction, and thence to Walsall; or by Prince's End *via* Wednesbury; or *via* Dudley Port to Walsall. The first route is 10 miles, the second 9¾ miles, and the third 11 miles, irrespective of junction detentions and change of carriages, whereas by the proposed Line the distance would be from Wolverhampton to Walsall 6 miles, thereby effecting a saving of 3¾ miles over the shortest present route, and without junction detentions or change of carriage. The saving of time between Wolverhampton and Willenhall, and Wolverhampton and Walsall would be even proportionately greater.

The Directors of the proposed railway have entered into arrangement with the London and North Western Railway Company, by virtue of which the new railway is to carry all traffic between Wolverhampton and Walsall and all the places between, all through traffic destined for Walsall, passing through Wolverhampton, and through traffic destined for Wolverhampton passing through Walsall, and also all through traffic arising at Wolverhampton or Walsall or intermediate places for which the proposed railway will form the shortest route. The traffic thus ensured to the Company, together with the traffic arising from a direct local communication between Wolverhampton and Walsall and Willenhall, and a direct through communication to places beyond Wolverhampton and Walsall will be necessarily very large. In addition to this traffic the new line will develop a mineral district in which, according to the opinion of the most eminent mineral surveyors, there are nearly 30 millions tons of ungotten coals and ironstone.

The London and North Western Railway Company will work the line and provide all the necessary Stock for 50 per cent. of the gross receipts, leaving the remaining 50 per cent. to be divided among the Shareholders of the new Company.

The population of the District comprehended by the Railway is about 250,000 and is rapidly increasing, and it is expected that the requirements of the traffic will justify the running of half-hour trains, and, in this event, a constant stream of intercourse will be maintained after the same manner as is established between Leeds and Bradford, Sheffield and Rotheram, and Kingstown and Dublin.

The experience of Railway enterprise has now proved that short direct lines between populous places, accommodating local traffic, pay the largest dividends.

The line has been laid out with every consideration of economy, combined with thorough efficiency, and the conveniences for local traffic have been carefully consulted.

The liability of the Shareholders is limited to the amount of their Shares.

Application for Shares in the accompanying form may be made to the Secretaries at the Offices of the Company, 66, Darlington Street, Wolverhampton; or to the Brokers; but no application will be entertained unless the deposit of £1 per share on the number applied for has been duly paid to the Company's Bankers; in the event of no allotment of Shares being made, the deposit will be returned in full, should a less number of Shares be allotted than are applied for, the deposit will be made available towards the payment on allotment and the balance, if any, returned to the applicant.

The second page of the Wolverhampton & Walsall Railway Company Prospectus.

National Archives

Little survives of the original WWR papers, but it would appear that there was no shortage of subscribers to the company, as it was authorized to seek loans for £40,000 on formation in 1865, increasing to £85,000 by 1870, but only £38,500 had been required at this latter date. The financial crisis caused by the collapse of the Overend & Gurney bank in 1866 had intervened, but it had evidently not seriously affected the company.

Although construction was delayed this seems to have been more to do with several changes to the route. Plans were deposited at Stafford County Court at 2.45 pm on 30th November, 1865 to include details of the southern approach to Walsall which were included in the 1865 Act, but not in the plans deposited in 1864. Also as no connection with the Stour Valley line was in the 1865 Act, a second Act was passed, on 23rd July, 1866 (Vict. 29 and 30, cap. 276) which specified that this connection was to be made at Crane Street Junction being '344 yards south of the booking office of Wolverhampton station'. The new connection (and a further minor deviation in Wolverhampton) were allowed two years for completion. The Act also empowered the LNWR to subscribe up to £100,000 towards the £220,000 paid up share capital of the company.

Later that year, on 29th November, 1866, plans were deposited at Stafford County Court (at 12.20 pm) reverting to the northern approach into Walsall, as given in the original plans of 1864. The company line would join the LNWR South Staffordshire Railway 'at a point opposite the centre of the pointsman's box for the junction of the Cannock and Rugeley Branch Railway with the main line of the South Staffordshire Railway' (i.e. at Ryecroft Junction). As a result a further Act was necessary to reflect these changes, which was passed on 12th August, 1867 (Vict. 30 and 31, cap. 180) Three years were allowed for completion, and failure to open in time for the conveyance of passengers would entail the forfeiture of the company's deposit of £604.

That same year further plans were deposited at Stafford County Court (on 30th November, 1867 at 12.30 pm) detailing minor changes to the alignment of the junction with the SSR at Ryecroft, and a further small change at Willenhall. A third change was the inclusion of a branch railway 'from 1 mile 5 furlongs on the WWR in field No. 132 belonging to John Edward Bealy, occupied by Isaac Bickley and terminating in premises of William Bradburn near to road passing over Wall Lane Bridge at spot known as "Farm Yard" in Wednesfield'. It ran from a junction on the WWR just west of the site of Wednesfield station turned 90 degrees to run north, then just after passing over the Bentley Canal reached a turntable, from where it faced west, then north-west into farm premises. These premises belonged to William Bradburn and actually were listed as a manure works. Further details of this small line will be found in Chapter Five. No Parliamentary powers were required for this line.

The 1867 Act had revealed a flaw in that the northern approach to Walsall would require two level crossings, which were unacceptable to the legislators, so a further Act was passed on 13th July, 1868 (Vict. 31 and 32, cap. 116) to authorize the company to construct a new road to replace the level crossings. The road was stated to be 'from a point where North Street and Portland Street unite, opposite Hatherton Street and Butts Lane in Walsall, and from thence carried over the SSR by means of bridge and shortly after that crossing diverging with one branch to

North Street and another to Portland Street'. This bridge still exists and carries the name of North Street as it crosses the railway. Four years were given for completion of the works, and the LNWR (as owners of the SSR, which the bridge also crossed) were allowed to contribute £2,000 towards the cost.

In 1869, further changes were afoot, being deposited at Stafford at 1.30 pm on 30th November of that year. This involved increasing the radius of the curve from Crane Street, Wolverhampton and three minor changes of alignment at Willenhall, Birchills and North Walsall. No legislation was necessary for these small changes.

As a result of the constant changes, time given in the preceding Acts for completion of the works was rapidly running out. So the company applied for an extension of time. This was first announced in the *London Gazette* of 7th December, 1869 that, 'A warrant by the Board of Trade dated 30th November 1869 in pursuance of The Railways (Extension of Time) Act, 1868 ordered and declared that the times by which the Wolverhampton and Walsall Railway Acts of 1865, 1866 and 1867 required the line to be opened to passenger traffic are to be extended by two years'. In actual fact, this is not quite what happened, as the company processed a further Act (Vict. 33 and 34, cap. 28) passed on 20th June, 1870 which uniformly extended the time given in the three Acts for acquisition of land to 20th June, 1871 and completion of the railway to 1st December, 1872.

Construction

Although there are no surviving records of the WWR detailing what construction work had actually taken place in the period from 1865 to 1869, it will be apparent that with the constant changes being made to the route, there was little opportunity to proceed firstly, with acquisition of land and property and secondly, with the actual construction work. Local newspapers of the time are also silent on these matters. Nonetheless, it is a fair assumption that little had been done on what is after all, only a six mile line, with no major works such as tunnels or river crossings to consider.

However, we do know that work had actually started prior to 1869, as in September of that year George Potter Neale notes in his seminal work *Railway Reminiscences* that 'inspection visits were paid with Mr. Addison the Engineer over the Walsall and Wolverhampton Railway'. But given the changes detailed above, it is unlikely that that much progress could be made until 1870/71, although presumably much of the necessary land and property had been acquired prior to this time (certainly it is confirmed that some lands were purchased in 1868).

No details are known of competitive bids submitted for the construction of the line, but the contract was awarded to the trustworthy Thomas Brassey, who had taken Messrs Ogilvie and Harrison into partnership for this work. It was to be one of Thomas Brassey's final contracts, and one that he would not see completed, as he died on 8th December, 1870. Mr Harrison was also the agent for contract, so he was in charge on a daily basis. As already mentioned, there is a lack of information concerning the performance of the works, but as there were little physical difficulties involved, it is presumed that work proceeded smoothly. Indeed, the lack of comment at the time reinforces this view.

The only comment worthy of note is from Thomas Brassey's own writing *Work and Wages* published in 1874 after his death:

> The recent increase in the demand for labour has produced a marked effect on the rate of wages on the Wolverhampton and Walsall Railway. Three years ago the navvies were paid at the rate of 2s. 9d. a day. Their wages are now from 3s. 6d. to 3s. 9d. a day ; and no more work is done for the money. Excavation is being made at a cost of 7d. a yard, which is thought to be dear work when the cost was about 4½d. a yard. The explanation of the present high rate of wages, is to be found in the fact that the railway in question is in the centre of the colliery districts, where the demand for labour in the collieries has caused a corresponding rise of wages for the workmen on the railway. Drivers, engaged at regular standing wages at the rate of a guinea a week on the Wolverhampton and Walsall Railway, are being attracted into the collieries by an advance of wages to the rate of 4s. 6d. a day. The same causes are producing the same effect on the Continent as in England.

It is known that several locomotives were used in the construction work. One such was the venerable *Gipsy Lass*, an inside-cylinder 2-4-0 built by Haigh Foundry, Wigan (Works No. 42) in 1840. This had earlier worked on the Midland Railway (MR) Leicester to Hitchin contract from 1854 to 1856, then on the Worcester & Hereford Railway contract from 1858 to 1861. After completion of the WWR it was advertised for sale on 20th/21st August, 1872, but its final disposition is not known.

A further locomotive believed to have worked here was *Rattlesnake*, an 0-4-0WT built (or possibly rebuilt) by Isaac Watt Boulton. It is believed to have arrived here in 1866, but returned to Boulton in 1867 (possibly because there was no work for it), then returned to the WWR and was offered for sale at the conclusion of the contract in August 1872. Again its final fate is unknown.

Inside-cylinder Manning, Wardle 0-6-0ST *Lincoln* (Works No. 266 of 1866) arrived here from Brassey and Ballard's MR contract from Bedford to Radlett around 1867, and afterwards in 1872 was sold to Exhall Colliery Co. Ltd at Bedworth in Warwickshire, moving at an unknown date to Awsworth Coal Co. in Nottinghamshire, after which nothing is known.

Two further locomotives may have been involved. One suspect was a tank engine built by George England of London and of unknown identity and arrangement. Another was a tank locomotive by James Cross of the Sutton Engine Works, St Helens.

Opening

Despite all the earlier delays, the line was opened one month before the Parliamentary powers elapsed, on Friday 1st November, 1872. As already indicated, it was worked entirely by the LNWR from the outset.

Two local newspapers covered the opening day, and gave an interesting insight into the initial passenger workings :

THE WOLVERHAMPTON & WALSALL RAILWAY

WOLVERHAMPTON AND WALSALL NEW RAILWAY
The directors of the Wolverhampton and Walsall Railway Company met at the offices, in Darlington Street, on Monday last (28th October), and from thence proceeded in a number of cars to the High Level Railway station, where a special train was waiting to take them along the new line. This was the final inspection previous to the opening of the line for general traffic on Friday next. The whole of the directors - who were accompanied by the engineer, Mr. Addison, and Messrs. H.H. Fowler, and J.E. Underhill, solicitors - were highly satisfied with the result of their inspection, and they accomplished the return journey from Walsall in about fifteen minutes, although only running at a moderate speed. The route of the new line, starting from the south end of the High Level (London and North-Western) Station, is through Heath Town, Wednesfield, Willenhall, Short Heath, Bentley, and Walsall. There are stations at all the places named, and, as at present arranged, there will be seventeen trains run daily to and fro between Walsall and Wolverhampton on week days, that is 9 from Wolverhampton, and 8 back. The first train will leave Wolverhampton at 7.10 a.m., and there will be 5 trains from that time to 12.15 noon, and 4 from 2-40 to 7.45. From Walsall there will be four trains in the morning (7.30 to 12.15), and four in the afternoon (from 2.35 to 8-45). There will be three fast trains each day from Wolverhampton, stopping only at Heath Town, Willenhall, and Walsall, and these will run the entire journey in 23 minutes. The other trains will stop at all the stations, and will occupy from 30 to 32 minutes on the journey between Wolverhampton and Walsall, and vice versa. On Sundays there will be three trains each way, the first leaving Wolverhampton at 9 a.m. The line will be worked by the London and North Western Railway company, subject to running powers over it by the Great Western and Midland Companies.
Wolverhampton Chronicle, Wednesday 30th October, 1872

The station at Willenhall was named Willenhall (Market Place)* upon opening, and the nearby LNWR station on the old GJR line was renamed Willenhall Bridge to avoid confusion.

Yesterday, the new line of railway Walsall and Wolverhampton was formally opened for the transmission of passengers. On Monday (28th October), the Directors, accompanied by Mr. Fowler (solicitor), Mr. Sutton (Birmingham) and Mr. Addison (the engineer), traversed the line from Wolverhampton to Walsall, and a dinner in honour of the event took place at the Star and Garter Hotel. According to the timetable, which came into operation yesterday, the service of trains daily will be seventeen in number, namely - From Walsall to Wolverhampton, 7.30am, 8.40, 9.50, 12.15pm, 2.35, 4.30, 6.55 and 8.45 ; from Wolverhampton to Walsall, 7.10am, 8.30, 10.10, 11.0, 12.15pm, 2.40, 4.10, 6.0 and 7.45. Three trains will run each way on Sundays.
Walsall Observer, Saturday 2nd November, 1872

As the new line took all the traffic on this route, the old route for LNWR passenger trains from Bescot via the GJR and reversal at Bushbury Junction was discontinued from the same date. The stations at Wednesfield Heath and Portobello closed to passengers from the following 1st January (1873). Not mentioned in either of these press reports is that goods services also commenced on the same date, but this is believed to be the case.

---

* Willenhall (Market Place) station was renamed as Willenhall in 1904, and renamed again, to Willenhall (Stafford Street), in 1924.

Working the line 1872-1879

The passenger services operated by the LNWR as indicated above, of nine up and eight down workings continued little changed during the period from 1872 to 1879. Two locomotives and sets of carriages would have been required, and due to the unbalanced times one empty stock working would have been necessary. The line was worked by block telegraph, and although it is not clear when this was installed, it is most likely to have been used from the opening.

Although the MR and GWR were granted running powers over the WWR in the 1867 WWR Act as from 1st September of that year, neither company is believed to have exercised these powers until 1875. Certainly, in January 1873 the only MR goods workings between Walsall and Wolverhampton was onSundays only leaving Burton at 5.30 am, pausing at Walsall from 6.50 am until 7.30 am then travelling via Bescot (reverse), along the GJR line to Bushbury Junction (reverse) and arriving at Wolverhampton at 8.15 am. It returned at 8.50 am by the same route arriving at Walsall at 9.50 am.

However, by January 1876 there was a daily weekday MR goods from Derby (3.40 am) arriving via the WWR in Wolverhampton at 8.40 am. The return working departed at 9.25 am. A further local goods service left Walsall at 8.05 pm arriving at 8.35, and returning at 9.50 pm.

It has erroneously been stated elsewhere that the LNWR and MR worked the line 'jointly' until the LNWR purchased the line. This mistake has been repeated in several publications, giving a warning that if a statement is repeated often enough it eventually becomes accepted as the truth. In this case, the evidence, as given above, is to the contrary.

Ownership of the line was about to change, and had been brought about by a number of factors, principally that the LNWR had not been abiding by the conditions of the 1864 agreement that they would carry all goods between Walsall and Wolverhampton on the WWR line. This had been occasioned by the opening of the SSR branch through Princes End as from 14th September, 1863. The LNWR eventually realised that this was a cheaper route for such goods (even if it was slightly longer) than via the WWR, where they would have to pay for travelling over the line. Furthermore, they had discouraged the MR from using the WWR (as indicated above), so that MR goods trains travelled over the LNWR lines (until 1874) and therefore paid the LNWR rather than the WWR. The MR had little say in the matter, as they had no goods facilities in Wolverhampton at that time.

The Board of the WWR were well aware of what was happening, and not just a little upset at relatively poor income anyway, decided after a number of objections had got them nowhere, to take the matter to court in 1873 seeking an injunction to restrain the LNWR from breaking its agreement. Unfortunately, for the WWR the decision of the Court was that an injunction could not be granted as the remedy was one of 'specific performance' (i.e. to order the way in which the agreement should be performed) and not an injunction (i.e. to prevent it from performing in any other way). So the action brought by the WWR was lost. Furthermore, the jurisdiction of the court was ousted by one provision in the agreement for reference to arbitration in the event of any dispute. This was further enforced by the provisions of the Railway Companies Arbitration Act,

1859 which referred such matters to arbitration. Arbitration eventually resolved the dispute to the satisfaction of the WWR, but relations with the LNWR had been seriously tarnished. Meanwhile, the LNWR was evidently a little wearisome of the necessity imposed upon it of keeping detailed records to prove that it was acting in the prescribed manner, and so offered to purchase this small company. This did not go down too well with some of the WWR Board members, and a faction led by the Chairman (still the Earl of Lichfield) proposed that the business should instead be sold to the MR. Meanwhile, the LNWR had included the vesting of the WWR in the LNWR as from 1st July 1875 in section 54 of its LNWR (New Lines and Additional Powers) Act (Vict. 38 and 39, cap. 152) passed on 19th July, 1875. The WWR Co. was dissolved as from this date.

Even though the line was now wholly in the hands of the LNWR, some dissatisfaction still surfaced. Passengers from Walsall and Willenhall were unhappy at the poor connections offered at Wolverhampton, and this is reflected in the following press report :

RAILWAY MANAGEMENT - A memorial to the chairman and directors of the London and North-Western Railway Company is about to be presented by the inhabitants of Willenhall complaining about the singular arrangements of the local traffic in its bearing upon the through traffic at Wolverhampton. At least in half a dozen instances during the day trains from Willenhall reach Wolverhampton just five minutes after the departure of a train from Wolverhampton to Stafford or leave Wolverhampton for Willenhall five minutes before the arrival of a train at the former place from Stafford and the North. It will be alleged in the memorial that, whoever is responsible for such anomalous arrangements, is substantially, albeit unintentionally, aiding the fortunes of the Midland Railway Company in the district. *Wolverhampton Chronicle*, 31st May, 1876

Prior to this time, the Act of 1872 had been passed for the construction of the Wolverhampton Walsall & Midland Junction Railway (WWMJR) line from Water Orton to Walsall, and we shall look at this in detail in Chapter Two. But the point here is that the MR had from that time been examining its presence in this part of Staffordshire. In section 36 of the MR (Additional Powers) Act, of 12th August, 1867 (Vict. 30 and 31, cap. 170) the MR had obtained running powers over the SSR lines of the LNWR , as well as over LNWR lines from Bescot to Wolverhampton (section 41) and over the WWR for Wolverhampton traffic only (section 46). We have seen that the MR had used these powers to operate goods services to Wolverhampton from Derby and Burton via Wichnor Junction and over the SSR line to Walsall and Bescot then via the GJR line to Wolverhampton – but that lack of its own goods facilities at Wolverhampton prevented any further expansion in this direction. At this time, it is believed that the MR had also to use the LNWR goods facilities at Walsall as it lacked its own there too.

Now committed to its new line into Walsall, the MR was looking to improve its presence at Walsall and Wolverhampton. By this time (1876) the LNWR had also not been idle and had resurrected the old 1847 plans for a line from the GJR at Portobello to Wolverhampton, which would connect first with the WWR at Heath Town, ½ mile from Crane Street Junction. Powers for the construction of this line, known as 'Wolverhampton Junction Railway', were eventually enacted in section 4 of the LNWR (New Lines) Act of 28th June, 1877 (Vict. 40 and 41, cap.

44). The line totalled 1 mile 2 furlongs 4 chains 30 links (1¼ miles). This Act also empowered the construction of a line of 1 mile 50 links (fractionally over 1 mile) from near James Bridge on the GJR to join the SSR line at Pleck, thus completing a new route directly between Wolverhampton and Walsall.

So it now suited both the LNWR and the MR for the line of the WWR to pass into the hands of the MR. This was accomplished by section 7 of the MR (Further Powers) Act of 11th August, 1876 (Vict. 39 and 40, cap. 209) vesting the line in the MR from 1st July, 1876. An arrangement was made between the two companies for the LNWR to continue to operate services until 31st July, with the MR taking over on the following day. The MR retained running powers into Wolverhampton High Level station. Section 9 of this Act also gave the LNWR running powers over the ½ mile of the WWR from Crane Street Junction to the point where their proposed line to Portobello would join.

To recap, from 1st August 1876 the MR had its own line from Walsall to Wolverhampton, but relied on the LNWR for passenger and goods facilities at Walsall and Wolverhampton. It also used running powers to operate over the LNWR (SSR) line from Wichnor Junction to Walsall, and had hitherto unused running powers onward to Dudley. Therefore, it also relied on its neighbour for the use of locomotive facilities at Walsall. Clearly, more needed to be done, and we shall examine this in Chapter Three.

Returning to the subject of operating in this period, it is evident that some improvement in passenger services was also required, and the MR soon set about this. By October of that year the frequency of trains on the WWR had increased from 8 to 14 up trains and from 9 to 15 down trains on weekdays, with three in each direction on Sundays. Of the weekday trains nine up trains and eight down trains stopped at all stations. Goods services remained the same at two daily weekday services, with some timing variations, as they were restricted by the use of the LNWR goods depot at Mill Street, Wolverhampton. However, in 1876 the GWR commenced a twice-daily goods service from Wolverhampton to Walsall (at 6.10 am and 6.20 pm) returning at 7.40 am and 8.20 pm. On Sundays there was one train each way leaving Wolverhampton at 6.00 am and returning from Walsall at 7.40 am. The GWR had taken a lease on part of the LNWR goods depot at Long Street, Walsall and it is presumed that their locomotives were serviced at the nearby original SSR locomotive shed.

Subsidence due to colliery workings was not an unknown problem for many lines, and especially in this area. The Way & Works Committee noted on 20th March, 1877 that a watch was to be kept for any potential subsidence in the vicinity of New Cross Colliery (between Heath Town and Wednesfield).

The Way & Works Committee awarded a contract for cleaning and painting stations on the line on 19th June, 1877 to T. Skevington in the sum of £171 2s. 4d., although no details are known of exactly what was required. Evidently this was fairly frequently required, as in 1882 a similar contract was awarded to the same contractor for £132 5s. 6½d.

The final change made to this line was the installation of a crossover at Heath Town Junction, in connection with the construction of the LNWR line from Portobello Junction. This was approved by the Way & Works Committee on 18th November, 1879 at an estimated cost of £380, and the work carried out soon after.

Chapter Two

The Wolverhampton Walsall & Midland Junction Railway

Formation and planning

Plans to construct the railway were deposited at Stafford County Court at 12.15 pm on 30th November, 1871 by the Engineer for the line, John Addison. The railway consisted of three lines:

No. 1 - the main line of 12 miles 1 furlong 7.25 chains (12⅙ miles) from a junction at Walsall with the Wolverhampton and Walsall Railway (then not completed) at Walsall North, to a junction at Water Orton, near Castle Bromwich with the MR near to a bridge over the 'fordrift' from Park Hall to Park Lane. The ruling gradient was given as 1 in 100.
No. 2 - a chord from the main line, a short distance east from Walsall North at a junction, running for 3 furlongs 5.50 chains (almost ½ mile) north to join the SSR at a junction near to Cart Bridge level crossing. Gradients were given as 1 in 82.15 for 3 furlongs, and 1 in 287 for the remainder
No. 3 - a chord from the main line, near to where the line crossed the Lichfield Road at Rushall (this point became known as Lichfield Road Junction) running south for 5 furlongs 3.50 chains (nearly ¾ mile) to join the SSR near to the level crossing of North Street (which became known as Ryecroft Junction). Gradients were shown as 1 in 158.85 for 0.2 furlongs, 1 in 100 for 4.8 furlongs and 1 in 400 for 0.2 furlongs.

The MR was to be permitted to contribute to the cost of construction.

The company to construct this line was incorporated in section 4 of its first Act (Vict. 35 and 36, cap. 182) passed by Parliament on 6th August, 1872. Time for completion of the railways was given as three years, and running powers were given to the WWMJR over the entire WWR, over the SSR from its junction into Walsall station, and over the MR to Nether Whitacre station. As the company was effectively sponsored by the MR it is not surprising that section 68 authorized entering into working agreements with the MR. On 12th December, 1872 the WWMJR made this formal agreement with the MR for them to work the completed line, and this was regularized in section 40 of the MR (Additional Powers) Act of 28th July, 1873 ((Vict. 36 and 37, cap. 210).

The first local reaction to the proposed line was one of horror that anyone should be permitted to desecrate the local beauty spot of Sutton Park by running a railway through it. This area had originally been part of Cannock Chase or Forest, and had been a royal hunting ground from the time of the Anglian Kings of Mercia. It remained popular with the royalty after the Norman Conquest from which time it had been the property of the Crown. In 1126 it was given by Henry I to the Earls of Warwick, although they never took up residence there. The 'Coldfield' part of the name of the nearby town of Sutton Coldfield is believed to denote the activity of charcoal preparation, common at the time in forested areas. Fishpools had been also established in the park, as a food source. However, circumstances changed when Henry VII granted Sutton Coldfield a Charter of Incorporation and relinquished his lordship of the manor, investing the manorial administration in a new corporation; 'the

This singular view, taken in the early 1920s, illustrates how the line bisected Sutton Park, much to the consternation of Birmingham residents. The view is facing towards Walsall, with the track running dead straight for 2½ miles. The tall signal is the up distant for Sutton Park station. *Author's Collection*

Warden and Society of the Royal Town of Sutton Coldfield', which included the park. By the 1820s most of the commonland had been enclosed, but was only frequented by relatively few people, as transport was both infrequent and costly. It only really became a popular area for recreation after the railway had been completed, and thus became easily accessible to the general population. So it can be claimed that the initial furore was simply not justifiable, and in any case the line of the railway as it passes through the park is softened by the planting of trees alongside. Nonetheless, the strip of land, some 2 miles in length as it traverses this section, was to cost the company some £6,500.

Just under a year later the WWMJR submitted a further Bill to Parliament, which was enacted on 7th July, 1873. This empowered the construction of a further railway at the eastern end of the line. This was for 5 furlongs 1 chain and 20 links ($^5/_8$ mile) running from the authorized line of the WWMJR at Curdworth near to Park Lane, southwards to join the MR at 790 yards west from the centre of the bridge over the aforementioned fordrift at Water Orton. Thus, it completed a triangle with the MR Birmingham-Derby line, so that traffic from the WWMJR could proceed northwards and southwards, and vice versa. Four years were given to complete this additional line.

Just a formality really, but the WWMJR was invested in the MR as from the passing of the MR (Additional Powers) Act, 1874 (Vict. 37 and 38) of 30th July, 1874. Section 31 of this Act gave these powers, and also authorized the dissolution of the WWMJR Company from that date.

Construction

The MR took over direct control of the construction project, and administered it through a 'WW&MJR Committee' at Derby. Fortunately, the Minutes of this committee survive and give us valuable insight into the construction. Firstly, the committee always referred to the line as the 'Walsall Branch', and at its first meeting on 17th August, 1874 confirmed the appointment of John Addison (of 4 Delaney Street, Westminster) as Engineer. Land purchase was a priority as powers were due to expire on 6th August, 1875. Two weeks later, the committee established Addison's rate of remuneration as being at £350 per mile, plus 5 per cent of contract value for drawings of stations and other structures. Addison asked for a further ½ per cent of contract value for drawings and calculations relating to the line, but was refused. The legal representative, W. Fowler, was appointed to purchase lands and property, and was remunerated at £30 per mile, excluding expenses - although later, on 5th November, he was awarded 5 guineas per mile for expenses.

Work proceeded speedily, and on 3rd November Addison reported that the plans were ready to be issued to potential contractors, so that they could prepare their bids for construction.

Tenders were received on 1st December, 1874 as follows:

	£	s.	d.
Thos Oliver	221,923	17	11
Burton Woodiwiss	201,947	12	3
Wall Brothers	201,289	13	0
Bayliss & Cropper	194,705	4	3
J. Firbank	171,906	7	5

The contract was awarded to Firbank, who, however, revised his tender on 5th January following to £171,882 5s. 10d. and the contract was issued in this amount. The Engineer's estimate for the line was £154,408 3s. 5d.

The committee meeting on 5th January, 1875 also confirmed that the line was to be laid for double track, and instructed Fowler to purchase land suitable for this formation. By 4th May, Fowler reported that land for the first 10½ miles of railway from Walsall (as far as Dead Man's Land, just past the Fazeley Canal at Minworth) had been purchased. Little construction work had yet been completed.

At the meeting of committee on 31st August 1875, the construction of 'a curve in the direction of Birmingham as pointed out by Mr Addison on plans was agreed to be constructed'. This is somewhat puzzling, as it presumably refers to the southern side of the triangle at Water Orton that was included in the 1873 Act. It seems unlikely that this was not included in the plans that were tendered by the contractors a year later, so perhaps there had been a reluctance to go ahead with this portion of the line at a earlier date, which was not recorded. More curiously, on 5th September, 1876 the committee decided that this new arrangement for a junction in the Birmingham direction required additional land, and confirmed that powers to do so were passed in the current Parliamentary session. In fact, these powers had been granted three years earlier.

Returning to 4th January 1876, land purchased at Walsall from the LNWR was reported to be 'in possession'. Work appears to have gone ahead without any major problems, as the next meeting was not until 1st August, when Addison reported that he had condemned ironwork for the line purchased by the contractor, and was instructed to obtain replacements at the contractor's cost. Furthermore, the contractor had complained that Addison had requested two piers in the middle of the River Tame to support the bridge, but that this would necessitate two coffer dams. The bridge was located on the northern side of the triangle at Minworth. This was obviously an expense that Firbank wished to avoid, and he had suggested a single span girder bridge as being adequate. This is the first intimation that relations with Firbank were not going smoothly. The committee decided to consider the matter at a later date, and on 3rd October decided that the two piers were necessary, but that they would award Firbank £400 for the cost of the two coffer dams.

At the meeting on 4th September, 1876, referred to above, Addison was instructed to communicate with James Allport (MR General Manager) as to where stations were to be sited, and what facilities were to be provided for passengers and goods. So evidently, work on the line was well ahead, and it was time to start thinking about the next stage. At this meeting, Addison also reported that his measurements of work completed did not agree with Firbank's measurements, which as these were used as the basis for interim payments, was a fairly serious matter. Addison was to report at the next meeting as to whether this disparity continued; however, nothing more was recorded for some time.

On 31st October, the committee was informed that the cost of land and the necessary easements for passing beneath the Birmingham Canal Navigation (BCN) Rushall Canal at Daw End would be £5,500. This particular piece of work was later to prove troublesome.

On 5th December, the committee met to consider 'a memorial from the inhabitants of Minworth soliciting the Directors to accommodate that village with a Station on the Walsall Extension Line'. The committee resolved to decline the request 'for the present', but in fact no such station was ever provided.

The committee were informed on 6th February, 1877 that sidings had been laid by the LNWR on some of the land purchased from the LNWR at Ryecroft in connection with the new engine shed being constructed there. However, by 6th March the LNWR had agreed to pay for this land.

On 28th June, 1877 the MR (New Works &c) Act (Vict. 40 & 41, cap. 52) was passed that authorized an extension of time (section 38) for the completion of the line for one year from 6th August, 1877. Actually, the previous time limit had already expired two years earlier and had not been legally renewed until this time. In any event, this extension was also to be exceeded without proper authorization, as the line did not open for passenger traffic until 1st July, 1879 - nearly one year late.

Work was evidently going reasonably well, for on Sunday 20th July, 1877 the committee went over the works, although there is no comment as to whether they found the work to be satisfactory.

Addison had prepared detailed plans for the stations and goods depots along the line, and these were examined on 4th September, 1877 having already been approved by James Allport. However, the committee decided that the schemes were too lavish, and referred them back to Addison and Allport for economies to be made. This matter was resolved when fresh plans were submitted to the committee on 6th November. These plans covered passenger stations at Aldridge, Jervis Town (Streetly), Sutton Park, Sutton Town and Penns, passenger sidings at Jervis Town, Sutton Park goods station and sidings and

Aldridge goods sidings. The details included buildings, platforms, goods sheds, cranes, weighbridges and offices, cattle docks and horse and carriage landings. The related estimates for construction were given as :

Aldridge	6,722
Jervis Town	2,869
Sutton Park	11,551
Sutton Town	7,647
Penns	4,904
Contingencies	1,307
Total	£35,000

These plans were approved, and on 5th February, 1878 Addison was authorized to obtain tenders from 12 contractors, although only four seem to have bothered to submit detailed tenders. These were:

	£	s.	d.
Lovatt, Birmingham	42,068	0	0
Wall Brothers, London	38,955	0	0
John Garlick, Birmingham	36,016	4	10
Jeffrey & Pritchard, Birmingham	32,175	5	3

A slightly revised Engineer's estimate was given as £35,082 18s. 4d.

The lowest tender, from Jeffrey & Pritchard, was accepted and the contract awarded. However, as might almost be considered inevitable, the plans for Aldridge goods and passenger stations, Water Orton Junction and sidings, and Sutton Park goods station were revised by James Allport on 30th April. These revisions were approved by the committee.

Returning to construction of the line, on 30th April, 1878 the final plan for the junction with the LNWR at Ryecroft was approved by the committee. Also, the earthworks for the chord running northwards near North Walsall to the SSR (Railway No. 2 of the 1872 Act) had evidently been completed, but the committee agreed that laying of permanent way materials should be postponed. As a result, no rails were ever laid on this section. The reason for the non-completion of this chord are not difficult to see, as the original intention would have been that traffic coming southwards from Wichnor Junction could access the WWMJR at this point. But with the imminent opening from Water Orton, such traffic would no longer need to travel over the SSR from Wichnor, thus saving the MR the expense of travelling over SSR (LNWR) metals. These earthworks, as they curve along the southern boundary of Ryecroft Cemetery have long perplexed observers, but can at last be explained. It was further resolved, on 4th June, that no statutory powers were necessary for the non-completion of the junction with the SSR near Cart Bridge crossing.

James Robinson McClean had used the trackbed of the SSR to lay water mains from the wells and works of the South Staffordshire Waterworks to Walsall and Wednesbury, which seems a remarkable use of resources - although he was also the prime mover behind both companies. The MR considered a similar scheme, and on 3rd December, 1878 considered a proposal from this water company to lay mains between Walsall and Sutton Coldfield. However, the committee turned down the idea, preferring to remain totally separate from any involvement with distributing water. Considering how many times our roads are disturbed to repair water mains, perhaps the committee had foreseen that such eventualities could disrupt traffic on their line.

Dissatisfaction with Firbank's work was probably behind the committee decision to record on 3rd January, 1879 that the MR was willing to take over the maintenance of the line, originally awarded as part of his contract. However, six months later Firbank was recorded as unwilling to release his maintenance contract.

On 6th May, 1879 the Board of Trade inspectors reported on their second inspection of the line. Subject to two or three minor matters, they approved the line for opening to passenger traffic. It is clear that Firbank had not completed all of the construction works, but whatever remained uncompleted was evidently not relevant to the opening of the line. Subsequently, on 3rd June, 1879 the committee instructed Addison to obtain not less than three quotes for work not done by Firbank. When completed, the cost of such work was to be deducted from payments to Firbank. The following month, Firbank asked for the balance on his account, which according to him was £107,133 0s. 9d. The committee declined this request, presumably because they were not yet in a position to determine how much they believed he was due. The opening of the railway went ahead on Tuesday 1st July, 1879 and details are given in the next section of this chapter.

On 7th September the committee examined tenders for the completion of Firbank's outstanding works. However, these were not complete tenders, but were based on schedules of prices because no statements of quantities were available at that time. No details were reported of these prices, but the tender of Lilley & Son of Ashby-de-la-Zouch was accepted.

It was nearly a year later, on 6th July 1880 that the committee received a claim from Firbank for the sum of £79,972 5s. 2d., being the difference between £401,878 7s. 3d. that he claimed was due to him and £321,906 2s. 3d. already paid to him. They were informed that a legal action had been started for this amount.

Firbank always maintained that the Engineer (Addison) had required additional work to be done, which he considered was not in the programme of works as outlined in the original plans, and from an engineering viewpoint was unnecessary. In particular, he considered the aqueduct carrying the Rushall Canal over the line at Daw End to have been one of the most difficult contracts he had ever carried out. Whether or not Addison had over engineered this or any other part of the line, it must also be considered that the BCN, as owners of the canal, would have required specific work to be performed, which Addison could have no influence upon. Canal owners had often become rather uncooperative when railway companies were constructing lines over, above or near their canals. One can have some sympathy with them as the railways were taking away the canal traffic, although the railway companies purchased many of the canal companies outright.

Firbank is known to have used three locomotives on this contract:

Sutton – was another Hunslet 0-6-0ST (works no.187 of 1877), coming new to this contract, hence its name. It possibly went next to Firbank's contract for the North Eastern Railway's Driffield to Market Weighton line, East Yorkshire from 1887 to 1890, then changed hands to work with the contractor William Arnold by 1898. By 1902 it was with William Rigby on work for the South East & Chatham Railway quadrupling of the

St Johns to Orpington line in Kent (1902 to 1904), then the extension of the Rother Valley Railway from Tenterden to Rolvenden (1904 to 1905), and reconstruction of Margate West station (1913 to 1914). Nothing further has been traced of its subsequent history.

Brighton – a Hunslet 0-6-0ST (Works No. 162 of 1876) sent new from Hunslet to the WWMJR on 13th April, 1876 carrying the name *Brighton*, suggesting that it was destined for Firbank's Brighton contract, but diverted to the WWMJR. After completion of its work here, it moved on 19th October, 1878 to Firbank's contracts for the London Brighton & South Coast Railway between Culver Junction and East Grinstead and from Haywards Heath to Horsted Keynes. Upon completion of these works in 1883, it was overhauled at Hunslet's works and next appears as being despatched to another contractor, Logan & Hemingway and in 1889 where it became their No. 5. It then passed at an unknown date to yet another contractor, Walter Scott & Co. as their *Darfield*. It was used on the 9½ mile MR Wath to Wrangbrook line between 1898 and 1899, then probably on the Lancashire & Yorkshire Railway's South Yorkshire line in 1900-01. It moved to work on the MR New Mills to Chinley Widening No. 2 in the following two years. By 1916 it was at the National Filling Factory at Chilwell, Nottinghamshire, but was for sale in June 1919. By April of the following year it was at Skipton Rock Co. Ltd in the West Riding. Its final disposition is not known.

Walsall – similarly this Hunslet 0-6-0ST (Works No. 188 of 1877) came new to this contract, then worked on the London & South Western Railway contract from Basingstoke to Alton between 1898 and 1901. In 1902 it worked on the GWR Acton to Ealing widening, then the LNWR Camden widening in the following year, then the GWR Clarbeston Road to Letterston and Goodwick widening and Fishguard Harbour contract in 1907. It was sold via the dealer C. Williams of Morriston, Swansea to Wm Lewis & Sons, Gorseinon Tinplate Works in 1908, which was its last known location.

In conclusion, Firbank may well have been a difficult man, and probably keen to ensure that he did not lose money on his ventures, but there is no evidence that he was not a competent contractor, as he had performed many contracts throughout the country. If he had been one of the 'rogues' his reputation would soon have seen him out of business. As it was, he died in 1886, leaving a personal fortune of £298,000. By today's standards this would equate to around £35 million.

Opening

As mentioned earlier, the line had opened for goods traffic on 19th May, 1879 and for passenger traffic on 1st July of that year. The local newspapers carried news of the event giving important detail:

> The Sutton Coldfield branch of the Midland Railway from Walsall to Water Orton, connecting the Black Country with the main line of the Midland system, will be opened for passenger traffic on Tuesday, July 1st, when excursions will run to Sutton Park Races. The Streetly Station is near to the raceground.
> *Wolverhampton Chronicle*, Wednesday 25th June, 1879

This is interesting, as the following accounts contained no mention of such excursions.

The second account was somewhat rambling, and only the relevant details are reproduced here:

The interesting and important event - the opening of the new branch of railway connecting Walsall and Wolverhampton with the whole of the Midland system - took place on Tuesday (1st July) morning last. Besides putting those towns in communication with one of the most gigantic systems in this country, it will also be the means of opening up new ground, and giving people an opportunity of reaching the pretty little and much-frequented village of Aldridge, and the spacious park and gardens of the royal town of Sutton ... The Midland had not a very cheerful day to open their new branch line, rain having come down nearly the whole night previous and at the time of sending the first lot of passengers on to Aldridge, Streetly, Sutton Park, Sutton Coldfield, Penns and Water Orton. The number of passengers was not very great, but this was to be attributed to the unfavourable weather. The first train on the time-bills was to start at 7.40, which it did to the second, the station-master of the London and North-Western Co. standing before the clock comparing notes with his watch, in order that there should be no mistake in the time. When the Midland carriages drove up to the platform, there appeared to be some hesitation about who should commence to call out where the train was going to. It was evident they had not had a rehearsal, and felt a kind of delicacy in making a beginning, being self-convinced that they would be looked upon as calling out 'Any more for Monday, Tuesday, Wednesday, and Thursday'. They certainly did not have that assurance about them which some of their peers possess at New Street station, who have the impudence to shout out, 'Any more for Walsall in England'. We were fortunate enough to get the first ticket which was issued for the new line, which was a third-class one to Aldridge. It appeared to be a bit of a novelty for the gent who doled them out made a remark as to whether the applicant intended to be the first to take a ticket for the new line. After the tickets had been examined, the train was not long before she steamed out of the station, to make the first ordinary run. The event had been anticipated, as several people were on the look out, but the only public recognition given to the train was by four bare-headed young urchins from Hawley's rope-walk in Cartbridge Lane, who waved their hats and shouted 'Hurrah!' as it sped along. The Blue Hole was reached in five minutes, and in another four minutes the ear was accosted with 'Aldridge, Aldridge'. There was no hesitation here (perhaps they had had a rehearsal), for before the train had stopped Aldridge was the all-absorbing topic dinned the ear. After looking round the handsome little station, which appears to be convenient as well as handsome, we took the first train back, which is timed to start at 7.51. As it was such a miserable morning, it was thought far enough to venture out, so we returned to Walsall, accomplishing the double journey in 23 minutes, including a change of train, look round the station, and getting a fresh ticket. This will be an improvement on the omnibuses, going to Aldridge and back for 6d., and in nine minutes. The Aldridge Coaching Company has done good service during the time of its existence, and has proved very useful and convenient to many who have no conveyance of their own to go to and from Aldridge. According to an advertisement in another column, now that the railway is open, the horses and omnibuses of the company are to be sold by auction on Monday week.

Walsall Observer, 5th July, 1879

The next report was rather terse – perhaps there were more important events that week on which to comment!

The Midland Railway – The new branch of this company's line from Walsall to Water Orton was opened on Tuesday with a good service of trains. The earlier ones carried but few passengers, but those in the middle of the day were well filled with visitors to Sutton races. *Staffordshire Advertiser*, Saturday 5th July, 1879

Block telegraph had been installed by the MR, and this method of working was adopted from the outset.

Chapter Three

Midland Railway improvements and expansion

Coincidental with the construction of the WWMJR, the MR planned to create large goods depots at Wolverhampton and Walsall, a locomotive depot at Walsall and a passenger station at Wolverhampton. The LNWR station at Walsall was under reconstruction at this time, and as part of that reconstruction the MR participated in the determination of what facilities it would require. Whilst that was relevant to the MR it was an LNWR project, so is out of the scope of this work. However, details of the works at Walsall station are contained in Chapter Six of my book *The South Staffordshire Railway – Volume 1* (Oakwood Press, 2010). The remaining major works are discussed below, although it will be evident that work was continuing on each of them at the same time.

Wolverhampton passenger station

Consideration had first been given to a passenger station in 1874, at which time the MR would have needed to exercise its running powers over the WWR to reach Wolverhampton. However, nothing more seems to have occurred at that time, although certain portions of land were acquired during the next two years. After acquiring the WWR in July 1876 the MR had no option at that time but to continue to use the LNWR High Level station for its WWR passenger services. Certainly, the MR plans for the land already obtained were at an advanced stage when the LNWR announced in 1876 that they intended to enlarge their own station, and that the enlargements would encroach upon the approach to the planned MR station.

The MR had resolved to build its passenger station near to the Wednesfield Road, at a site almost alongside the eastern side of the GWR Low Level station. However, the LNWR plans to extend their High Level station would have cut off their approach road from the town centre, also used by the GWR. The town council had supported the LNWR plans, and proposed that the MR station should be sited on land already acquired by the MR near to Bailey's ironworks. However, this was not acceptable to the MR, as they argued that passengers would have a very convoluted journey from the town centre to such a site.

The matter was referred to arbitration at the House of Commons before a Select Committee, and this was reported in the *Wolverhampton Chronicle* of 12th July, 1876 as follows:

THE LONDON AND NORTH-WESTERN RAILWAY (NEW LINES) BILL
House of Lords, Tuesday
The existing station of the London and North Western Company should be altered, and for that purpose a street situate between the High Level Station and the Low Level Station of the Great Western railway should be acquired from the Wolverhampton corporation, who should receive for it the sum of £10,000: that this street should be

stopped up : and upon it lines constructed for goods traffic, and further accommodation be given to the passenger stations, the platforms of which would be widened, and other improvements made. The opponents were ... the Midland Company, who as proprietors of the Wolverhampton and Walsall Railway, contended that the proposed alteration would stop up a means of access to the passenger station which they intended to construct. The latter would, however, still have a more direct route by Cornhill and Mill-street to Five-ways, which was the converging point of all the streets of Wolverhampton ... He (Mr.Pope, for the promoters) submitted that what was proposed would be of no detriment to the Midland Company, that it would largely benefit the public ...

The natural and most direct route for traffic to the Midland Station would be by Mill-street and Cornhill ... The site which the Midland Company had bought for passenger and goods stations, was a far better site for a passenger station than the piece of land near Bailey's works, which was now suggested.

House of Lords, Wednesday
Mr J. Addison CE was examined in further support of the opposition of the Midland Railway Company ... In 1874 he and Mr Allport went over the ground with him ... He reported in favour of the site which it was alleged would be affected by the Bill, as being the only site for a good passenger station. If the station was placed on the site indicated by Mr Underhill the Midland Company would get no passengers at all ... It was not necessary for the LNWR to stop up the road altogether ... another alternative was the construction of a colonnade, which would cost about £12,000 ...

Eventually, the LNWR enlargements were not permitted to encroach on the approach road that led to Corn Hill and the town centre, and the MR was permitted to continue to use the LNWR station (running powers having been granted to the MR under their 1867 Act). As a result, the MR applied for permission to redevelop the roads in the area, so as to improve the approach to their proposed station. This was noted in the *Wolverhampton Chronicle* of 15th November, 1876:

MIDLAND COMPANY'S EXTENSIONS AT WOLVERHAMPTON
Parliamentary sanction is sought to be obtained by the Midland Company to make a new road, commencing at Far Sun-street, which is at the western end of Bayley-street, and terminating on land belonging to this company, which lies between the high and the low level lines of the Wolverhampton and Walsall Railway, abutting on Sun-street, more popularly known as Sloppy-lane. The company proposes to purchase property adjoining and near to and on the south side of their Wolverhampton and Walsall Railway, near its termination at Wolverhampton, and lying between that Railway and the Wyrley and Essington Canal ; and also certain other lands, houses, and buildings adjoining, and near to and on the north side of the said railway, near its termination aforesaid, and lying between the said Railway and the Wednesfield-road, to stop up and discontinue all rights of way over the existing footpaths which now cross the last-mentioned lands, and to make in lieu thereof a new footpath, commencing from and out of Sun-street and Lower Sun-street at their point of junction, and terminating by a junction with New Sun-street at the western end thereof. It would appear that the Midland Company's intention of erecting their new passenger station in this locality is not to be abandoned, despite the adverse criticisms of the Town Council expressed when the scheme was first mooted.

Note that the land mentioned as lying adjacent to the Wyrley and Essington Canal was that eventually used for the MR Canal goods depot (*see below*). The application was successful and the various roads referred to as Sun Street are those which exist today.

However, the LNWR was evidently not happy about sharing its High Level station with the MR and notified them on 30th June, 1878 that their running powers into the LNWR station would cease in one year. As Parliamentary powers had been granted for the running powers under the MR Act of 1867, this unilateral pronouncement seems a little heavy-handed, if not unlawful. The MR appealed against this decision, and negotiations with the LNWR successfully concluded an extension of the running powers.

Meanwhile, the MR had proceeded with its plans for the new station, and at a meeting of the MR Board on 5th June, 1878 had notified their South Construction Committee to purchase land for the erection of the station. Their Engineer, John Underwood was to produce a land plan. The WWMJR Committee reported on 2nd July, 1878 that all the required adjacent land from the GWR had already been acquired, and any remainder would be purchased by private treaty. A month later, James Allport reported to the same committee that the plans for the passenger and goods stations were completed, and these were approved by the committee.

On 4th March, 1879 tenders were received and examined for the passenger station building:

John Garlick & Co.	£3,558	19s.	8d.
P. Horsman & Co.	£3,420	0s.	0d.
Engineer's estimate	£3,040	0s.	0d.

From these sums it would seem that the station would have been a rather modest affair, of certainly no more than two platforms, and would be included as part of the site of what became the Wednesfield Road goods depot. The committee made no decision at this time, postponing consideration for the time being. Certainly the MR would only have needed a modest station, as they could not hope to compete with the LNWR and GWR on routes to London. Any northwards services could connect with the MR system at Burton, Derby or Leicester and so need only to be of modest proportions.

However, the renegotiation with the LNWR for the continued use of their station (which was in a much better position relative to the town anyway) rendered these plans superfluous, and so plans for the new MR station were dropped. It is interesting, however, to peruse the Ordnance Survey map of the Wednesfield Road goods yard, for even in later years there are earthworks for a double line on the western side of the yard that were never laid with track. These were at a higher level than the rest of the yard, so would give trains an easier start on the climb to the WWR main line at Heath Town. This site was also in such a position as to be near to the Wednesfield Road and alongside Sun Street for passenger access to and from the town centre. Therefore, it is suggested that work on the passenger station proceeded to the point of preparing the earthworks for the lines, at which time the idea was dropped.

A view of Wednesfield Road goods depot building in January 1979, clearly showing the three hipped-roof sections running for the length of the structure. At the facing end are the entrances for the three internal rail tracks. On the left side of the building is the substantial canopy over the loading area for road vehicles. *S. Dewey*

Wednesfield Road goods station and yard around 1956, with a considerable amount of activity, as two unrecorded former LNWR 0-8-0s are engaged in shunting. The MR passenger station would have been sited to the left centre of the picture, on the line occupied by a string of wagons curving into the distance. The GWR 'Siphon' and LMS parcels van in the foreground have been stabled on the chord connecting to the GWR line. On the right, part of the yard has been taken over by a scrap merchant, whilst the large building in the left background is the GWR carriage shed adjacent to the Low Level station. *R.S. Carpenter Collection*

Wolverhampton goods depot

As mentioned above, plans for a goods station at Wolverhampton were submitted by James Allport to the WWMJR Committee on 6th August, 1878, and approved. However, on 1st October next they were revised, and John Underwood estimated the cost to be £20,200, of which £13,670 would be for building work to be let by contract. Earthworks, fencing, footpaths and bridges could be done by schedule totalling £4,500. The remainder, mostly ballasting and permanent way would be done by the company. If required, a grain warehouse would cost a further £5,500. Further land at Wolverhampton had been acquired from Charles Evans & Co.

On the following 5th November tenders were examined by the committee:

	Goods station			Goods yard		
	£.	s.	d.	£	s.	d.
Engineer's estimate	15,005	4	3	9,130	0	0
C. Perkins				9,527	14	11
J. & G. Tomlinson				9,998	17	5
J.R. Lovatt				10,188	9	11
J. Hartley	14,511	3	8			
J. Garlick	15,021	16	4			
Lees Brothers	15,038	13	3			
Jeffery & Son	15,219	13	8			
W. Cox	15,445	4	7			
J. Parnell & Son	15,699	8	8			
J. Robertson	15,856	0	0			
C. Claridge	15,994	0	0			
John Wood	16,227	13	8			
Jones & Co.	16,360	15	3			
Henry Lovatt	16,500	0	0			
Wm Moss	16,584	10	8			
Dawson & Co.	16,806	14	0			
P. Horsman & Co.	16,874	18	3	7,763	0	0
Geo. Lilley	17,425	6	0			
R. Mason & Co.	17,909	4	2			
J.T. Tatlow	18,850	15	8			
Rowley & Lynex	19,892	12	0			

J. Hartley's tender was later withdrawn. The tender of John Garlick of Birmingham was accepted for the goods station building, and for P. Horsman & Co. for the station yards.

It was noted that cottages on land purchased would have to be removed. One month later, on 3rd December, it was noted that works had already been commenced, and the three old cottages had been removed, with the materials therefrom being sold to the contractor, P. Horsman for £350.

Work proceeded well and in May 1879 Underwood reported that the fencing under the bridge for a footpath was nearly ready, as was the cattle dock and about half of the earthworks were done. The main building was nearly five feet above the ground. Quantities were reported one month later as being 5,277 cubic yards of earthwork for the goods yard and lines, 214 cubic yards of brickwork, 1,281 cubic yards of metalled roads in the yard, and 581 cubic yards of permanent way. At the beginning of July, it was reported that the earthworks should be completed by the end of the month and that 'ballasting in roads and yards was in hand'. A further month elapsed when it was reported that the roof for the goods station had been delayed by the late delivery of ironwork, but that the earthworks for the goods yard were nearly finished and all ballasting in a 'forward state'. Permanent way was expected to be laid in September, which duly commenced on time. Weighing machines were to be supplied by the MR stores and locomotive departments. The committee made plans to inspect the works in November 1879 and found that the permanent way had been laid in the yard. At the end of the month, the goods station was being finally roofed, and one month later was nearly complete.

On 1st January, 1880 the committee examined tenders for further work, this time for the construction of stables for 17 horses and 3 looseboxes. Such accommodation would be necessary for the horses required to deliver goods from the new depot.

Engineer's estimate	£1,375	0s.	0d.
Lilley & Son, Ashby	£1,287	5s.	1d.
E. Wood, Derby	£1,384	8s.	0d.
J. Garlick, B'ham	£1,397	0s.	7d.
Pritchard & Co, Birmingham	£1,411	7s.	4d.
Jeffery & Son, Birmingham	£1,490	0s.	0d.
H. Lovatt, Wolverhampton	£1,531	9s.	8d.
Moss,Wolverhampton	£1,560	8s.	10d.
Horsman & Co., Wolverhampton	£1,573	0s.	0d.
W. Cox, Leicester	£1,632	19s.	3d.

Being the lowest, the tender of Lilley & Son was accepted.

At the meeting on 3rd February it was reported that the goods shed roof was now complete, and all permanent way laid except into the goods shed. It was expected that the entire project would be completed in April, but by 1st June the signals for the junction had still to be completed, which was considered to be the final stage. The committee inspected the yard and buildings on 20th July, 1880 and recommended that the site could be taken over by the Way & Works Committee, which meant that it was then ready for traffic to commence.

The official opening date is given as 4th October, 1880, but it is highly likely that the facilities would have been in limited use prior to this date.

The building measured 217 ft by 66 ft and was of two storeys, constructed of red brick, with the roof being divided into three hipped sections running its length. Three rail lines ran through its entire length, and on emerging at the far, northern end, adjacent to Wednesfield Road, were given pointwork to enable the transfer of wagons from one line to another. On its western side, four large doorways enabled the transfer of goods to road vehicles, which were protected by a cantilever canopy running almost the whole length of the building on that side. On the eastern side there were just two loading platforms for road vehicles, with smaller cantilevered canopies provided at these apertures.

Alongside this, road vehicles were also loaded and unloaded direct from wagons in the sidings sited here. Cattle pens were sited alongside the most easterly of the sidings on the eastern side of the site. At the end of the building facing the road entrance, a smaller and lower two-storey hipped roof extension (overall 80 ft by 28 ft) provided office accommodation and mess rooms for the goods depot staff. Further groups of two sidings were added with two groups on the western side of the yard, and three more groups on the eastern side. From a central point in the yard, another pair of sidings led off to the north-west, passing alongside a 50 ft turntable. These sidings were used for coal traffic, wagons being unloaded directly by the local coal merchants. Apart from water columns, the turntable was the only other facility provided for locomotives. It is not known when this turntable was taken out.

A small signal box was sited in the centre of the yard, but almost certainly functioned as an enclosure for a ground frame, although communication with Heath Town Junction box would have been necessary.

The rather steep rail entrance to the goods yard from Heath Town Junction did mean that one restriction was applied to all loose-coupled goods trains, in that they had to come to a stop at Heath Town Junction for brakes to be pinned down before descending into the goods yard. In addition, a 20 mph speed restriction applied to this line and to the chord to the former GWR line.

The depot continued in use by the MR, London Midland & Scottish Railway (LMSR) and British Railways (BR) (under whom it became known as Wednesfield Road goods depot until 1966, after which the site was leased to Railstores Ltd. However, little use was made of the building until their lease expired in October 1988, by which time the entire area was decidedly derelict. Meanwhile, the area formerly occupied by the coal sidings was designated as a coal concentration depot in 1964. With the downturn in demand for coal, this facility was closed in November 1983, and was afterwards taken over by a local scrap merchant, adding to the run-down appearance. But in 1988 the depot was given a new purpose, becoming an overflow for the Wolverhampton steel terminal located on the site of the former GWR Walsall Street goods depot. By 1990 it was receiving two trains per day (one from Redcar with steel from Lackenby, and one from Scunthorpe) so that around 1,000 tons of steel was unloaded daily, for storage and eventually onward movement. However, this was not to last, and the site was eventually completely cleared around 1994 for the erection of a new Royal Mail sorting office.

Wolverhampton Canal goods depot

The majority of the heavy goods traffic such as coal, coke, iron ore and finished and semi-finished iron and steel products were transported to the iron and steel works, foundries and gas works by canal, and had been done so for over a century in some cases. However, many of these businesses were not rail connected (and some never would be), and so the MR recognized that with suitable transhipment, they could still offer a faster delivery than having these commodities transported entirely by canal. Such a need was obvious in

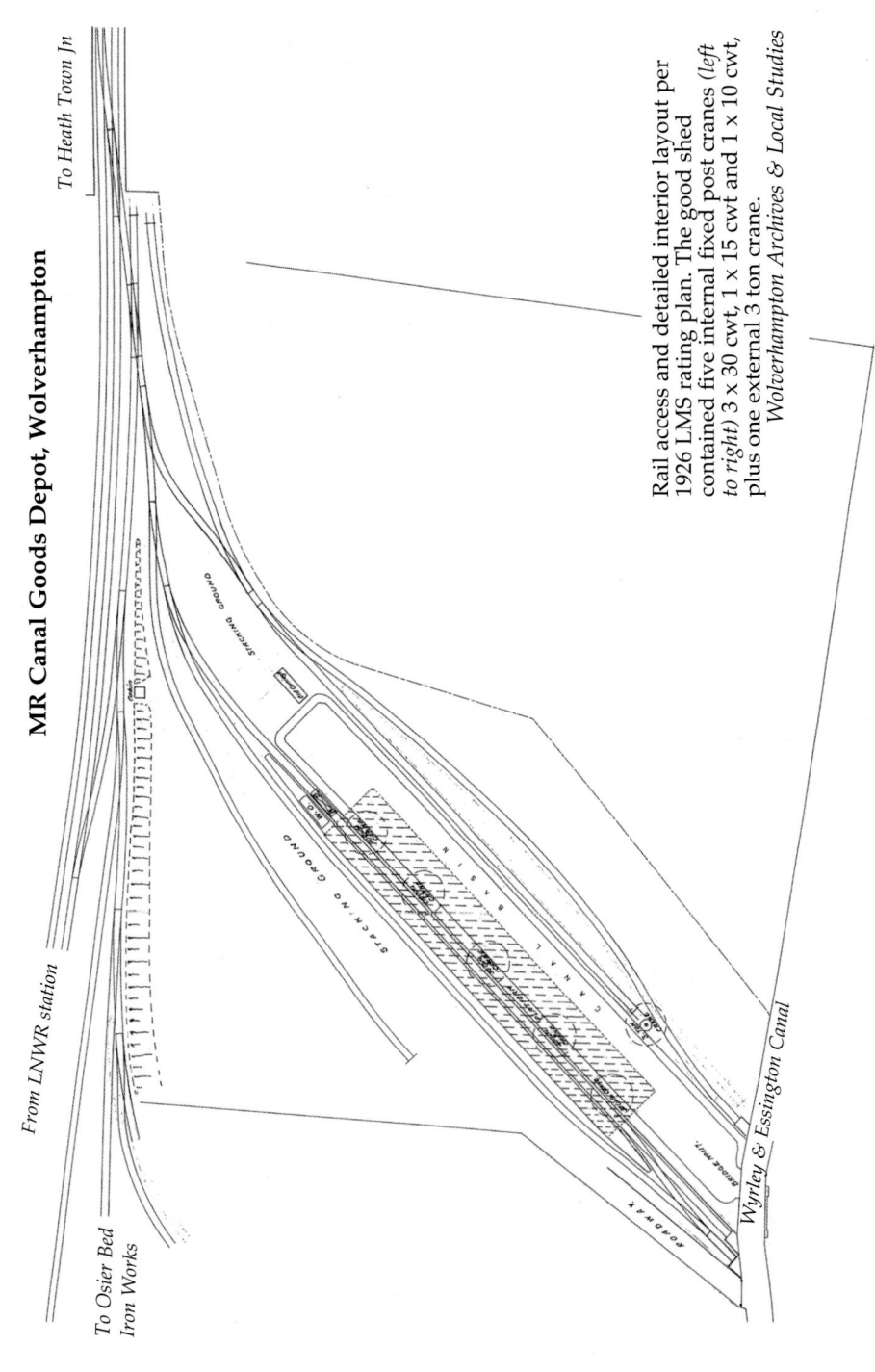

MIDLAND RAILWAY IMPROVEMENTS AND EXPANSION

Wolverhampton and the MR had acquired land, including an unused basin adjacent to the Wyrley & Essington Canal, on the south-western side of the WWR during 1865 and 1875. This site was also adjacent to the Osier Bed Ironworks, to which the WWR had already laid a connection.

On 18th January, 1881 the Way & Works Committee requested that 'a plan and estimate be prepared for providing a siding and canal basin at Wolverhampton as per sketch submitted at an estimated cost of £13,000'. Just two weeks later this committee was informed that the plan and estimate had been prepared, giving an estimate of £11,000, exclusive of any further land required. This was referred to the General Purposes Committee for approval, who granted this on 15th July following.

A schedule of works and tender for £2,500 was received from Henry Lovatt and approved by the Way & Works Committee on 31st January, 1882 for constructing the canal dock. However, on 5th April the committee was informed that it would be necessary to purchase further land totalling 4,991 square yards at an estimated cost of £4,991 plus a public house.

The former MR Canal goods depot in Wolverhampton was still in operation in 1955, when this view was taken, looking towards Heath Town Junction. The single road beneath the canopy extended over the canal basin to protect goods and workers during transhipment.
R. Selvey Collection

On 16th May approval was given to Henry Lovatt's tender of £4,200 for the construction of a goods shed at the canal basin. Then on 31st May, it was approved that in order to make a direct rail entrance to the canal depot rather than a curved one, it would be necessary to purchase a further 790 square yards of land from the Osier Bed Iron Co. at £1 per square yard. This was also approved.

Work appears to have been made rapidly, for on 3rd October the committee approved the purchase of a 10 ton crane (estimate £360) and weighing machine (estimate £228) for the site, although this was not approved by the General Purposes Committee until 5th December. The final stages of work recorded are gas fittings (£121 9s. 1d.) approved on 20th March, 1883 and telephone communication (estimate £42) to connect to the main goods station on 4th May, 1883.

So it would appear that this canal side structure opened for traffic some time in the Spring or early Summer of 1883. Of course, just as for the other goods depots, the opening of such a lowly structure would not and did not merit inclusion into any local press reports.

The goods shed provided covered facilities for the transhipment of goods between railway wagons and canal narrow boats. It partly covered the basin and was 20 ft high and 300 ft long, having solid oak roof trusses with cast-iron support columns, and a slate roof laid on timber laths, with a central double row of roof lights in the apex. The internal platform was partly solid and partly laid with timber beams on a brick foundation. On the northern end of the depot was a rail weighbridge made by Messrs Pooley Ltd which had a capacity of 40 tons. To simplify the transfer of goods, the rails were laid relative to the canal so that the floor of the rolling stock, the platform, and the gunwhales of the narrow boats were at the same height.

Under the LMS it became known as Wolverhampton Canal depot, but attracted little traffic in the 1920s and gradually fell into disuse and decay. Although it survived the war, by 1960 the site was almost totally overgrown. Around 1969 the site was purchased by the adjacent Wolverhampton and Birchley Rolling Mills Ltd (successors to the Osier Bed Iron Works Co.) and the goods depot was demolished. The site was redeveloped for the expansion of the rolling mills, so that the only trace remaining today is a small bridge alongside the Wyrley & Essington Canal over the canal arm that led into the Canal Depot basin.

Walsall goods depots

The MR had relied on the LNWR for its goods facilities at Walsall up to 1876, but after taking over the WWR, was under pressure to make its own arrangements. During that year it started to plan its requirements. A meeting was held with Walsall town council on 27th November, 1876, which was reported in the *Wolverhampton Chronicle* of 29th November :

MIDLAND RAILWAY IMPROVEMENTS AND EXPANSION

THE MIDLAND COMPANY AT WALSALL

On Monday night, the chairman of the Midland Railway company (Mr Ellis, MP), and the general manager (Mr Allport), solicitor (Mr Beale), the engineer (Mr Addison), had an interview with the Walsall Town Council, sitting as the General Purposes Committee, for the purpose of explaining a bill which the company intend to promote in the next session of Parliament to enable them to acquire the whole of the Lammas lands and a piece of land belonging to Lord Bradford, to construct a branch line out of the present station belonging to the London and North-Western Railway company, on to the Lammas lands, and to erect on such lands new passenger and goods stations. They stated that they were under an agreement with the London and North-Western company to find station accommodation within 18 months, and they trusted that the Council would assist in the matter, particularly as to the acquisition of the Lammas lands. A general discussion followed, in which a feeling very favourable to the Midland Company was shown, and a disposition also to provide a public recreation ground or people's park out of the proceeds of the sale of the Lammas lands. In the end a resolution was passed to the effect that in the opinion of the Council additional railway and station accommodation are necessary for the town, and that, subject to considerations in detail, the Council will assist the Midland Company in the furtherance of their proposed plan.

Statutory powers were necessary for the construction of the branch leading to the goods yard and were contained in section 4 of the MR (New Works, &c.) Act passed on 28th June, 1877 (Vict. 40 & 41, cap. 52). The branch was to be 3 furlongs 7 chains 10 yards long (a little under ½ mile) from a junction with the LNWR to Long Meadows also known as Walsall Lammas Lands.

Work in progress on the modernization of the former MR goods depot at Walsall during 1962. The original fabric of the building can be seen, with the cast-iron arched window surrounds, partly obscured by the new cladding being applied.   *R. Selvey*

There seems to have been some delay in obtaining the required lands for it was not until over year later, on 1st October, 1878, that the WWMJR Committee were informed that the estimated costs for the new goods depot would be £33,500 of which buildings would cost £10,195, and earthworks, fencing and roads £13,000, both to be let by contract. The remainder would be performed by the company, and some £1,500 by the LNWR.

At the meeting on 5th November, 1878 the tenders for construction were examined (at the same time as those for Wolverhampton, given above):

	Goods shed			Iron traffic shed		
	£.	s.	d.	£	s.	d.
Engineer's estimate	9,098	16	11	1,228	4	2
Lees Brothers	8,713	11	1	1,110	17	3
J. Garlick	8,774	0	0	1,343	0	0
Jeffery & Son	8,990	12	0	1,240	14	10
J. Hartley	9,103	15	0	1,202	2	0
Dawson & Co.	9,179	0	0	1,596	0	0
John Wood	9,287	16	5	1,387	11	8
J. Parnell & Son	9,292	18	10	1,328	17	2
W.Cox	9,330	15	4	1,431	12	0
J. Robertson	9,485	0	0	1,318	9	8
Wm. Moss	9,531	2	1	1,584	4	1
C. Claridge	9,542	0	0	1,437	0	0
Jones & Co.	9,803	14	7	1,423	19	10
Henry Lovatt	10,000	0	0	1,400	0	0
Horsman & Co.	10,073	4	6	1,520	10	1
Geo. Lilley	10,306	15	10	1,495	13	2
R. Mason & Co.	10,862	15	10	1,812	16	4
Rowley & Lynex	13,533	7	5	1,612	4	11
J. Cooper				2,779	1	7
	Station yards					
Engineer's estimate	13,480	0	0			
P. Horsman & Co.	12,648	4	8			
J. & G. Tomlinson	13,131	3	4			
J.R. Lovatt	16,320	14	4			

Contracts were awarded to J. Garlick of Birmingham for the goods shed, to Lees Brothers for the iron traffic shed and to P. Horsman & Co. for the goods station yards.

These contracts had commenced by the following month, and six months later, on 6th May, 1879, the committee were informed that excavation and formation of the goods yard and a new road was about half completed. The goods shed was about six feet above the ground and the iron shed was ready for slating. The following month this was translated as 5,311 cubic yards of earthworks, 127 cubic yards of brickwork, 155 cubic yards of concrete, 576 cubic yards of stonework, 500 cubic yards of ballasting for permanent way, and 196 cubic yards of metalled roads. The goods shed was in a forward state, and the iron shed almost complete. Just four weeks later the new road and Tasker Street were two-thirds complete, and good progress being made on all other parts.

By August the warehouse was ready for its roof and the embankment for the goods yard was ready for ballasting. Earthworks for the sidings and connection to the LNWR had commenced, and boundary walls were partly done.

The November inspection by the committee visited Walsall as well as Wolverhampton and found the yards ready for permanent way. The goods shed was complete, and in February 1880 the permanent way was being laid. On 1st June it was reported that only the signals needed to be installed, and the following month it was recommended that the Way & Works Committee should take over the site. In August 1880 a temporary junction had been installed, so that the goods yard and depot could be used.

The goods shed was a single-storey brick-built structure with but a single road passing through. Although an altogether smaller structure, the 'iron goods' shed was sited further south and faced north. It had two roads passing through, but much less storage space, as presumably most of the 'iron goods' could be stored outside. Although the two goods sheds were treated as one depot, the main depot was sited near to Midland Road and the iron goods shed next to Tasker Street, and so became locally known by these names, officially being redesignated as such at a later date, probably by the LMS after the Grouping in 1923. Both depots remained in use by the LMS and BR until the area alongside Midland Road was redeveloped for the new goods depot in 1962, at which time they were both demolished. A new goods depot was opened on this site on 7th October, 1962 and cost £500,000. It was intended to serve as a concentration depot for 26 towns in the area between Oldbury and Lichfield covering around 250 square miles. However, the move away from railborne wagonload freight made the depot redundant, and it was used for the storage of permanent way vehicles. Eventually, in 2000 the building was taken over by the English Welsh & Scottish Railways Ltd (EWS) as a parcels depot, but this too became redundant, and the site has been cleared awaiting redevelopment.

A signal box was positioned at the entrance to this yard, on the up side of the line just north of the Corporation Street bridge, opening with the goods yard. This was replaced by a standard MR hipped-roof box on 27th August, 1905, which lasted until 3rd January, 1927.

Walsall engine shed

The MR seems to have been a little slow to realise that with the opening of the WWMJR line, additional locomotive servicing would be required. So it was not until 30th September 1879 (two months after the WWMJR had opened) that the General Purposes Committee decided that accommodation for 12 engines would be required. Underwood had prepared an estimate of £14,923 for the works and was instructed to obtain tenders for the work. These were submitted to the WWMJR Committee for consideration just over a month later, on 4th November (the preparation of the yard was split into two sections):

	Yard preparation						Engine shed erection		
	Schedule 1			Schedule 2					
	£.	s.	d.	£	s.	d.	£.	s.	d.
Engineer's estimate	4,012	19	11	4,401	5	5	7,609	11	10
J. Garlick	2,710	5	1	4,724	0	9	7,352	5	6
J. Evans	4,900	11	0	3,715	0	8			
J. Wood							7,563	15	10
G. Lilley & Son							7,682	1	7
E. Wood							7,735	0	0
Jeffery & Son							7,759	8	9
Pritchard & Co.							7,780	11	8
J. Robertson							7,974	6	11
W. Cox							8,104	10	8
P. Horsman & Co.							8,277	0	0
Purnell & Co.							8,845	17	3
H. Lovatt							9,036	16	8
W. Moss							9,125	10	5

John Garlick was awarded the contracts for all three phases of the work.

It was reported during March, April and May 1880 that work on all aspects was proceeding well, and that the yard would be partly ballasted in June. This was accomplished, with the permanent way being laid the following month. At their meeting on 31st August, the committee was informed that the engine shed would be ready for use in early September, and it duly opened for business during that month.

The MR had laid its own independent lines from the goods yard for about ½ mile further south to just short of the Wednesbury Road overbridge, where the locomotive shed was sited. It was a three-road engine shed, with a standard MR wooden coaling plant approached by a lengthy ramp for the coaling trucks, and a 50 feet diameter turntable in the yard. It was generally known as Pleck shed, but locally it was also often referred to as New Mills. The building measured 220 ft by 48 ft, and was constructed of red brick, with a single gable-ended slated roof. All three roads terminated inside the building, although one was originally planned to pass through. Alongside, and next to the main running lines were three carriage sidings. The parent depot for the shed was Saltley (3A), and so Pleck was coded '3B' in MR days. As might be expected, following the Grouping much rationalization took place, and the shed closed on 2nd September, 1925, its allocation moving to the former LNWR depot at Ryecroft. However, that was not the end for the building, which was thereafter used for carriage storage and maintenance, lasting well into BR days in this role. Rakes of 12 coaches for excursion traffic were regularly stabled in the former locomotive yard. The building fulfilled a different role for the duration of World War II, when it was requisitioned for the storage of aircraft radio and electronic equipment. Eventually in the 1970s it became redundant, and was left empty for several years whilst a further use or potential lessee could be found. However, it caught fire in 1984, and was subsequently demolished as being in a dangerous condition. The site remains unused.

Chapter Four

Other railways

As might be expected, a number of schemes were promoted in the area that intended to use running powers over some or all of the WWR and/or the WWMJR. None of them were ever successful, in fact none ever proceeded beyond the promotional stage. Many such promotions were purely speculative, with the hope of selling out to larger railways once they had obtained running powers over their rivals. Others hoped to build at least part of their lines, then sell them on to the larger companies. Some did actually hope to build their own lines, even if it meant that they would have to have the larger companies operate them. Although the larger companies were quite capable of building any lines they wanted, this latter option was often attractive, as it meant that they would not risk their capital if the line proved to be unprofitable. Then if the line was profitable, they could purchase it (as occurred with the WWR), and be in a strong position to negotiate the price. Just to illustrate the number of such schemes, those traced are listed below, although there may have been even more:

Birmingham Dudley Wolverhampton Walsall & Tamworth Railway Co.
Dudley Wolverhampton Tamworth Syston & Leicester Railway Co.
Dudley Wolverhampton Walsall and Tamworth Railway Co.
Leicester Tamworth Walsall, Wolverhampton and Shrewsbury Junction Railway Co.
Lichfield Walsall & Wolverhampton Railway Co.
South Staffordshire & London Railway Co.
Tamworth Walsall & Wolverhampton Railway Co.
Wolverhampton Birmingham & Nottingham Railway Co.
Wolverhampton & Nottingham Railway Co.
Wolverhampton Walsall & Atherstone Railway Co.
Wolverhampton Walsall & Dudley Railway Co.
Wolverhampton Walsall Leicester Peterborough Norwich & Great Yarmouth Junction Railway Co.
Wolverhampton Walsall Lichfield Tamworth Ashley & Nottingham Railway Co.
Wolverhampton Walsall Stamford Peterborough and Norwich Junction Railway Co.

It is not proposed to go into any further details regarding these schemes, which did not mature into incorporation nor did they gain an Act of Parliament. However, there were four local lines that were promoted, and were designed to join the WWR at differing points.

WWR Extension

Plans for this line were deposited at Stafford County Court at 3.30 pm on 30th November, 1865, just five months after the WWR had been authorized and incorporated. It was to run for a further 2 miles and 5.10 chains (just over 2 miles) from a junction with the proposed WWR at Clarke's Lane, Short Heath turning north-east and eventually joining the SSR Cannock line at 198 yards south from the centre of Bloxwich station. Running powers were then necessary

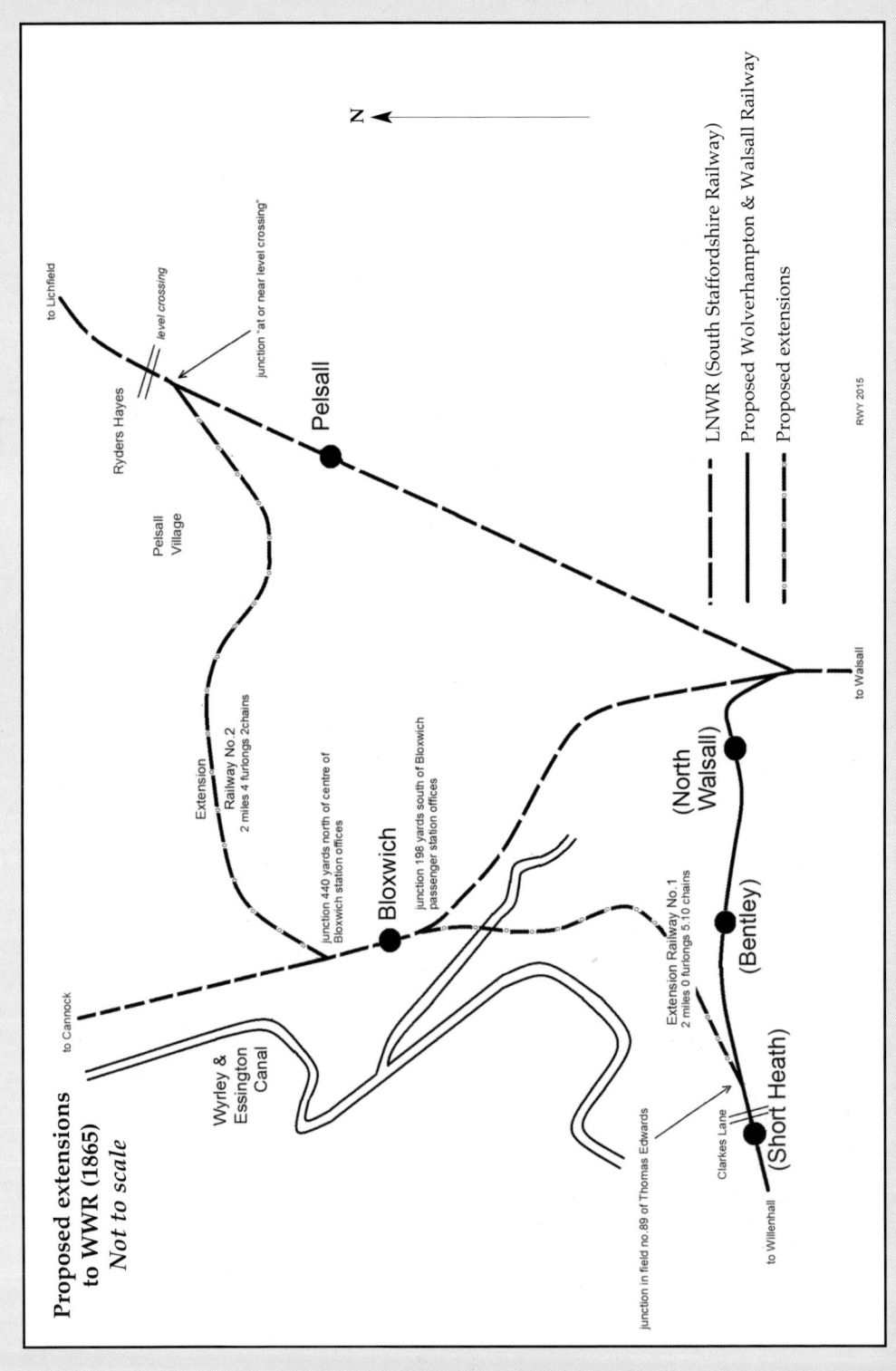

over the SSR to a junction 440 yards north from Bloxwich station. From here the new line continued for 2 miles 4 furlongs 2 chains (2½ miles) eastwards passing to the south of Pelsall village and joining the SSR Lichfield line just south of the level crossing at Ryders Hayes.

The intention was clearly to attract traffic from the north on to the WWR, eliminating the necessity for reversal in Walsall. However, this line was well beyond the financial capability of the fledgling WWR, and so a Bill for Parliamentary powers was never processed.

WWR Bentley branches

Plans for these lines were deposited at Stafford County Court at 10.55 am on 29th November, 1873. Railway No. 1 was to run from 300 yards east of the centre of Short Heath station (in field No. 223 on the tithe map) at a junction, for 1 mile 4 furlongs 9.50 chains (about 1½ miles). It terminated in field No. 242 alongside the southern side of the Wolverhampton to Bloxwich road in the parish of Bentley. The ruling gradient was given as 1 in 118.

Railway No. 2 was to run eastwards from a junction with Railway No. 1 at 6 furlongs from the commencement of that railway for 3 furlongs 7.80 chains (just under ½ mile). This crossed the Wyrley and Essington Canal and terminated alongside that canal on its far side. The line was level for almost all of its length.

The intention of this line was to serve several coal mines in the area, and also to connect them with the Wyrley & Essington Canal. The proposed Bill for this line would have enabled the LNWR to construct the line, but at this time relations with the LNWR were somewhat strained, so it was withdrawn and the railway never proceeded further.

Wednesfield & Wyrley Bank Railway

The line was promoted as being 4 miles 6 furlongs in length, from a junction at Wednesfield. This was an independent company, striving to link the collieries in the Essington and Wyrley area to the WWR line. No deposited plans have been traced, but an Act was passed on 19th July, 1875 (Vict. 38 & 39, cap. 143), which incorporated the company. It also authorized the line to run for 4 miles 6 furlongs (4¾ miles) from a junction with the WWR at Wednesfield to Great Wyrley. No mention is made of a junction with the SSR at Great Wyrley. Time for construction was given as five years, and the company was authorized to enter into working agreements with the LNWR.

There was no progress whatsoever with the line, and it was proposed in 1877 that the company should be amalgamated with either the LNWR, MR or even the GWR. It would appear that the company was short of funds and desperate for a buyer. Nothing more seems to have occurred, and a public notice in the *Wolverhampton Chronicle* of 12th, 19th and 26th November, 1879 recorded that a Bill for Abandonment would be lodged at the Houses of Parliament before 20th November. That Bill was enacted on 29th June, 1880 (Vict. 43 & 44, cap. 15) authorizing abandonment of the railway and the dissolution of the company.

42 THE MIDLAND RAILWAY ROUTE FROM WOLVERHAMPTON

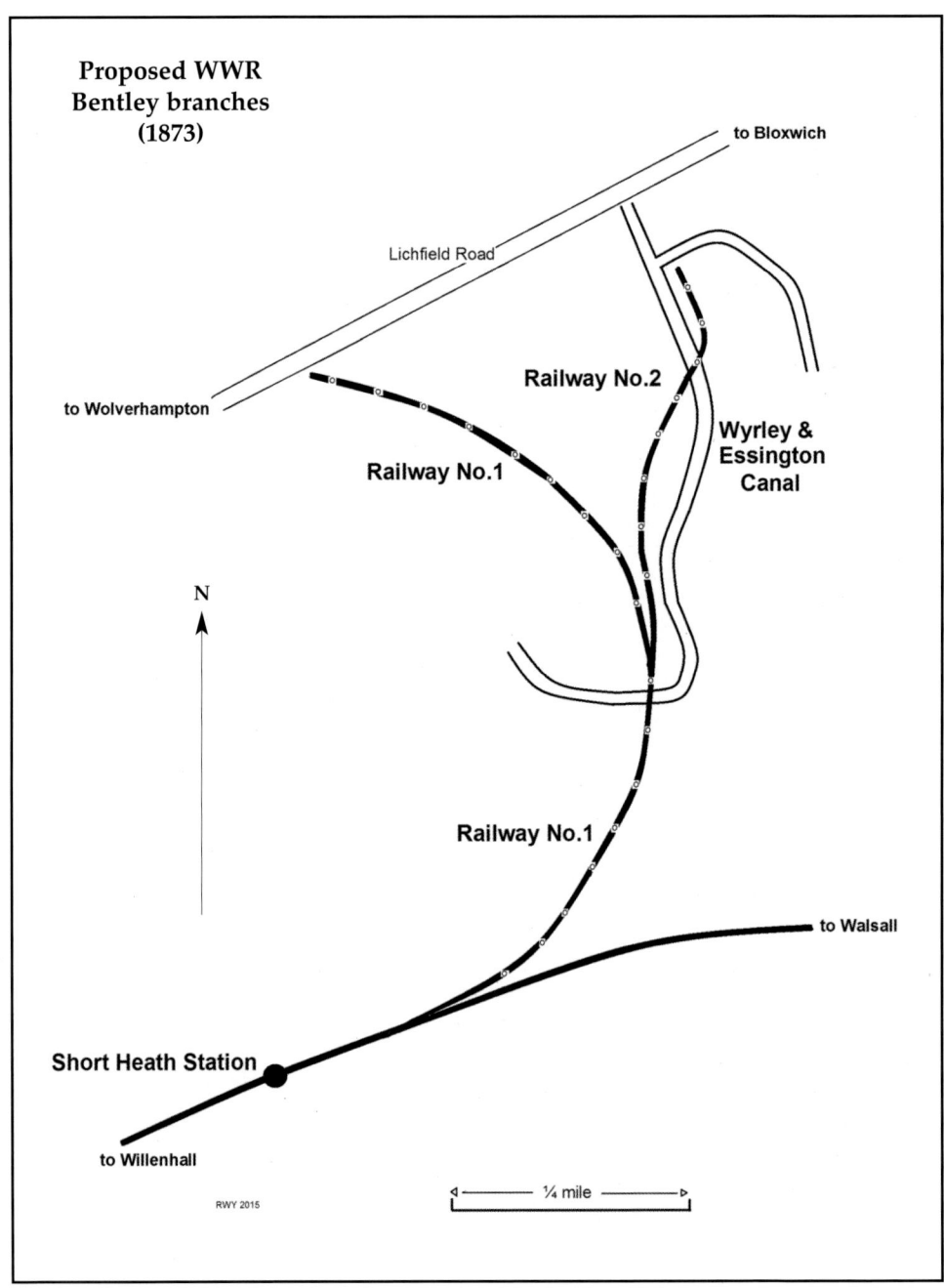

Essington & Ashmore Light Railway

Plans for this light railway were deposited at Stafford County Court on 25th November, 1898. The line was promoted by the Directors of the Holly Bank Coal Co., who had earlier been thwarted in their attempts to promote the Wolverhampton & Essington Mineral Railway and then the Wolverhampton & Cannock Chase Railway in 1898, which would have given them a connection to the main line railways in Wolverhampton. This new line was to consist of three railways:

Railway No. 1 - ran south for 1 mile 6 furlongs 3.50 chains (1¾ miles) from a junction on the private line near to Holly Bank Colliery at Essington, east of Bursnips Road. Just east of Ashmore Park Farm, it passed Ashmore Lake on the west side, turning east to terminate on the northern bank of the Wyrley and Essington Canal near to Broad Lane. It was to be double track for all of its length apart from a small siding at the eastern end.

Railway No. 2 - was for a double track line of 1 mile 5 furlongs 5.30 chains (1¾ miles) from an end-on junction with Railway No.1 just east of Ashmore Park Farm and before crossing the Wyrley and Essington Canal. It was to run to a junction with the WWR about ½ mile east from the WWR bridge over Clarke's Lane, Short Heath.

Railway No. 3 - was a single track line from a junction with Railway No. 2 north of its junction with the WWR, then turning south and passing beneath the WWR using an existing under bridge. As it neared Darlaston, it was to turn east and run parallel with the GJR line, which it was to join at Darlaston Green sidings, about midway between The Crescent and Bentley Road at Darlaston.

Costs of construction were estimated by engineers Pritchard & Co. as being £25,039 (Railway No. 1), £15,732 (Railway No. 2) and £15,605 (Railway No. 3) for a total of £56,376. The Light Railway Order was passed on 29th January, 1900 and authorized construction of this standard gauge line within five years. Maximum axle weight was given as 14 tons and maximum permitted speed on the line was 25 mph. Running powers were given to the company over the entire WWR, and over the GJR line into Bescot station. Working agreements were to be permitted with the LNWR and/or the MR.

However, the LNWR objected to this line and so these plans were amended on 23rd November, 1900. Railway No. 1 now changed direction, making a junction at Essington (thus facing towards the colliery) turning south and crossing Sneyd Lane to Bloxwich Road where it terminated. Thus it was slightly shorter at 1 mile 1 furlong (just over a mile) and was to be laid as single track. Railway No. 2 was divided into two sections, so that the new Railway No. 2 was only 5 furlongs 3.45 chains (just over ½ mile) and was single track running south-westerly as it passed Ashmore Lake. The second part became the new Railway No. 3 and continued from Railway No. 2 for just 5 furlongs 5.60 chains to terminate on the south side of a minor road. Thus no connection was then to be made with the WWR. Railway No. 4 was a short (1 furlong 5.10 chain) siding running northwards from a junction with Railway No. 3 near Spring Lane to Sneyd Coppice near Knight's Bridge over the Wyrley & Essington Canal.

Evidently, without a main line connection, the company failed to achieve its objectives and the powers were allowed to lapse. Sections of the proposed line from Essington to the Wyrley and Essington Canal at Coltham were eventually utilized by the Holly Bank Colliery Company as a private line in 1924.

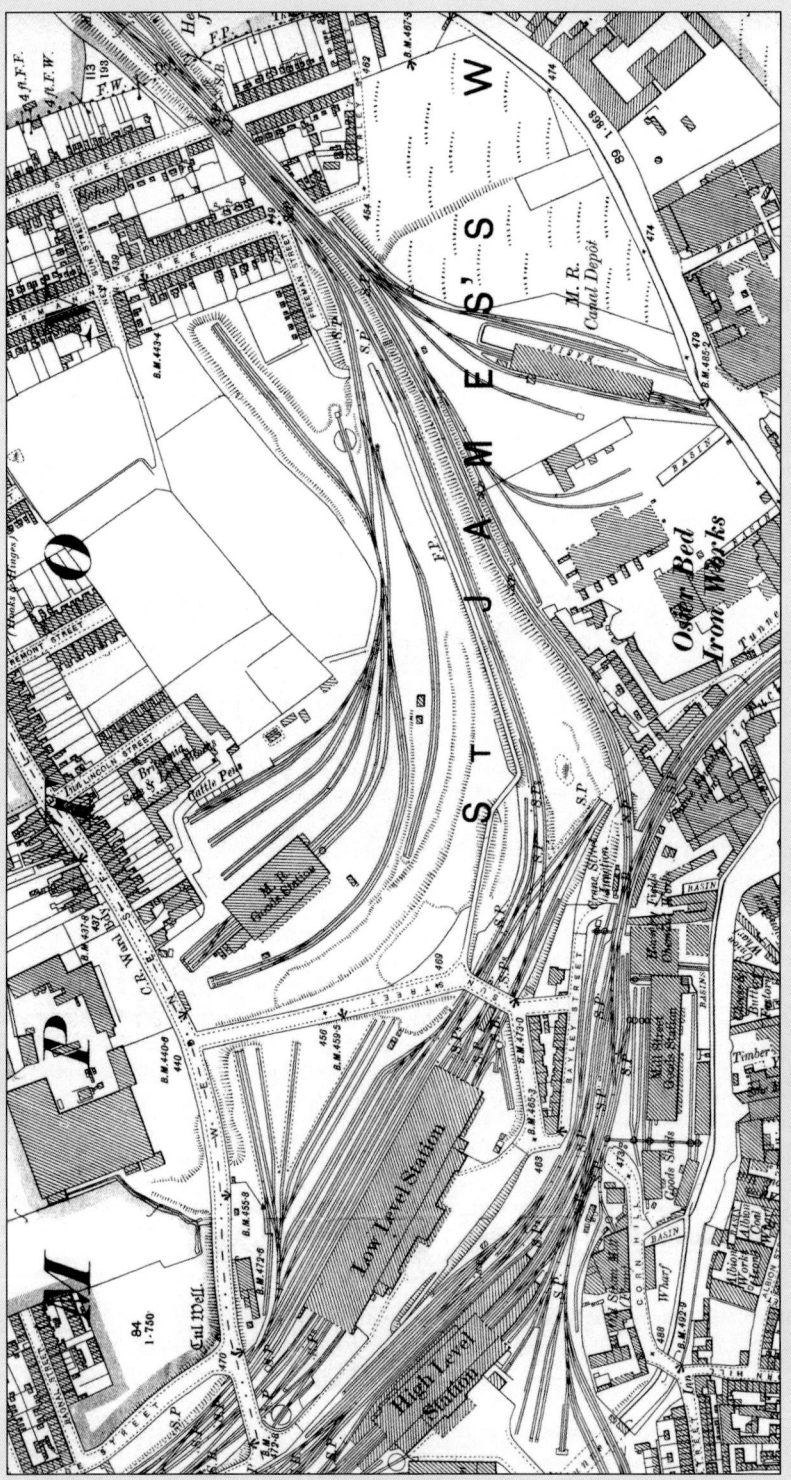

Wolverhampton showing the Wednesfield Road MR goods yard and depot in the centre, with the turntable off to the right of the yard. The site of the proposed passenger station lies to the left of the goods depot building on the embankment with earthworks shown continuing from the two short sidings (later removed). The MR Canal depot is in the lower centre of the map.

Reproduced from 25 in. Ordnance Survey map, 1883

Chapter Five

Description of the Line

Starting at the western end of the line, this chapter describes the line and the many features of interest, both operational and visual as they appeared during its lifetime. Mileages quoted are from Crane Street Junction.

Wolverhampton High Level station was firstly known as 'General' station, and opened on 1st July, 1852. It was originally planned by the Birmingham Wolverhampton & Stour Valley Railway, but this company was leased by the LNWR in late 1846, who thereafter determined the construction. The Shrewsbury & Birmingham Railway (S&BR) had contributed half of the cost of the station, and used it from its opening until the S&BR was absorbed into the GWR in 1854. Towards the end of that year, the GWR Low Level station opened (to which the S&BR had also contributed one-third of the cost) and so the former S&BR trains ran into that station. Actually, the High Level station acquired the name Queen Street station from September 1853, as the station entrance originally led from this town centre thoroughfare, and although this designation officially lasted until 1st June, 1885 the station had colloquially become known as 'High Level' for some years. From that date it officially became 'High Level', which name continued until 7th May, 1973 when it became simply 'Wolverhampton', as there was no need to distinguish it from the former GWR station which had closed completely in the preceding year.

The station buildings were an attractive variation of Gothic revival and executed in stone. The original station entrance building stood at the end of Queen Street, from which a driveway took passengers to the station proper. This entrance building was later to fall into disuse, but survived several attempts at demolition and still stands today as a monument to the city's history, albeit now surrounded by a bus station and other modern developments. The station proper soon became regarded as inadequate as traffic increased and the meanness of some of the facilities were often criticized locally. By 1876, as we have seen in Chapter One, although the LNWR had been moved to reorganize the station layout, their efforts to expand towards the GWR station were limited by arbitration. The original layout provided just one platform for each direction, with a subway connecting the two. The waiting room on the up platform was considered to be inadequate, and the platforms considered too narrow. Goods lines passed to the east, behind the up platform.

Rebuilding did not commence until 1884, as amongst several other factors, a new street had been built (Lichfield Street) which lined up the centre of the town directly to the station forecourt. When completed in 1885, the new station was renamed and consisted of a lengthy down platform, with bay platforms at each end for local trains terminating from the north and south. Up services were provided with an island platform on the eastern side, and a foot bridge connected the two. This was situated beneath a plain overall iron canopy with glass roof panels spanning the central portion only of the two platforms. Platform canopies were later added at each end of the two platforms, thereby

Wednesfield Road goods depot, Wolverhampton in rather heavy snowy conditions in January 1979. The goods depot building was still in reasonable condition at this time. *S. Dewey*

The SLS special of 22nd June, 1963 that toured various lines in the West Midlands is seen here leaving Wolverhampton Low Level behind LNWR 0-8-0 No. 49361, and taking the chord built as part of the original link with the WWR main line at Heath Town Junction. The WWR main line running from the LNWR at Crane Street Junction is on the top of the embankment directly above the locomotive and leading three coaches. The works beyond are the Birchley Rolling Mills. *Author's Collection*

Parcels vans being transferred by 350 hp 0-6-0DE No. 08783 from the former Wolverhampton Low Level station, by this time in use as a parcels concentration depot, in the wintry conditions of January 1979. *S. Dewey*

increasing the area under cover. Goods lines continued to pass to the east of the station.

This station remained virtually unaltered until electrification, when reconstruction began in February 1964 and was completed in time for the commencement of the new electric services on 6th March, 1967. This work had involved the complete removal of all station buildings and replacement with modern structures, all done whilst maintaining passenger services. The platform and running lines were largely unaltered, and having lost its overall roof the public became once more aware of the lofty and windy situation of the station. Subsequent improvements were made in the 1990s with the addition of a further platform on land previously used by the goods lines, but this is really proceeding too far ahead, and it is time we moved along.

The line runs southwards, passing the LNWR Mill Street goods depot on the right, almost immediately reaching Crane Street Junction, where the WWR forked off to the left on a blue-brick viaduct that carried it over the tunnel of the GWR line to Birmingham Snow Hill. At this divergence the substantial works of the Osier Bed Iron Works were situated, which were connected to the WWR a short distance further on. This company passed into the hands of John Lysaght Ltd in 1885, becoming the Wolverhampton Steel & Iron Co. Ltd in 1916, reorganized as the Wolverhampton Steel & Iron Co. (1946) Ltd in that year and then nationalized in 1947. It returned to private ownership in 1955 as the Wolverhampton & Birchley Rolling Mills Ltd. In 1963 the works were acquired by Stewarts & Lloyds Ltd, being nationalized once more in 1968 and becoming part of the British Steel Corporation. Until 1970, shunting was performed by steam rail cranes, but from that date the various owners used their own locomotives (*see Appendix One*) for the movement of rail traffic to and from the WWR exchange sidings up to the takeover by Rotherham Engineering Steels Ltd in 1988. At this time the sidings were taken up, although for some time there had been no inward or outward rail traffic, and the locomotives were used purely for internal movements of steel. After acquisition by Corus plc, this works closed in 2009.

Now descending at 1 in 100 on a substantial embankment, next on the right came the former Canal goods depot, already described in Chapter Three. Meanwhile, over on the left the double track chord connecting to the GWR line just south of Wolverhampton Low Level climbed up to meet firstly, the line into Wednesfield Road goods depot, at a point some 100 yards before the LNWR Portobello line diverged off to the right at Heath Town Junction (½ mile). A further 100 yards later, the double track line from the goods yard joined the WWR on the left. As a consequence of the siting of the junction for the Portobello line, trains from that direction could not run directly into or out of the Wednesfield Road goods depot and the spur to the GWR. Instead, in later years, any such workings had first to set back down the WWR line before reaching the access. Meanwhile the Portobello line ran parallel with the WWR for about 200 yards. These two junctions formed part of what became Heath Town Junction, which was controlled by a signal box, initially on the eastern (down) side of the line. This was replaced as from 19th May, 1912 by a box on the opposite side of the line, which closed on 15th August, 1965.

48 THE MIDLAND RAILWAY ROUTE FROM WOLVERHAMPTON

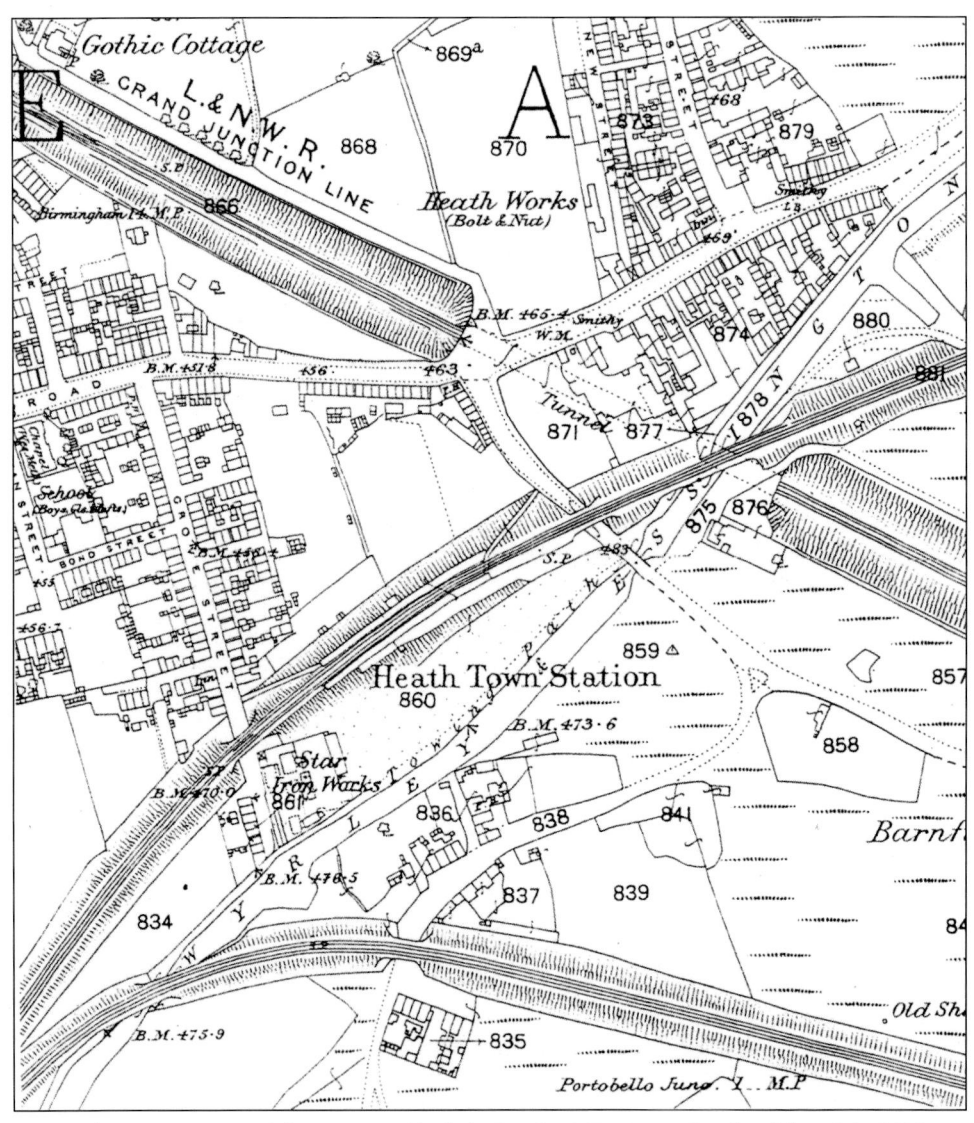

Heath Town station, and the crossing of both the Wyrley & Essington Canal and the original GJR route near Deans Road.
Reproduced from 25 in. Ordnance Survey map, 1889

After passing rows of terraced houses and the erstwhile Alma Brick & Tile Works on the left, the line entered **Heath Town** station (¾ mile), situated on the lofty embankment. This station was a fairly simple affair with just one platform on each side of the line and had only a relatively short life. Lengthy and quite steep footpaths connected to Deans Road and Grove Road on each side of the line. There were no goods facilities, and the exact construction of the station buildings remain a mystery as no photos or plans of it have been traced. It had opened with the line, and was used primarily as a ticket platform - there being little in the way of local passengers owing to its closeness to Wolverhampton. Ticket platforms were in widespread use by the LNWR, as their practice was to operate many principal stations as 'open' stations and the checking of passengers' tickets took place at the station immediately preceding the principal station. Wolverhampton was one such example, where the LNWR also established ticket platforms at Bushbury Junction to the north, and Monmore Green to the south on the Stour Valley line to Birmingham. However, it became clear that in some circumstances the holding of trains at these locations seriously disrupted services by occupying track space on congested lines. This was certainly the case at Monmore Green, limited by its double track and only slightly less so at Bushbury Junction. The rather less intensive traffic on the WWR would not have been a problem, but in the light of the change to a 'closed' status at High Level in 1910, all ticket platforms were abolished and so this station was closed as from 1st April of that year.

The line continued in a north-easterly direction, first crossing Deans Road then the Wyrley & Essington Canal, both on blue-brick skew bridges. At this exact point the canal also crosses the GJR line from Bushbury to Portobello which was in a short tunnel. From here the line gradually turned more easterly, still running on an embankment and falling at 1 in 100. There were numerous collieries in this area, and narrow gauge tramways passed beneath the line serving the pits, landsale yards and spoil heaps at Deans Colliery (G. & R. Thomas Ltd), at Bowmans Harbour Colliery (Whitehouse & Poole) and at New Cross Colliery (H.B. Whitehouse & Son).

Approaching Wednesfield, a single track came in from the north and then ran parallel with the WWR to a junction. This line was mentioned in Chapter One as having been included in plans deposited in 1867 for a line of 1 furlong 6 chains (just under ¼ mile) to run alongside Backhouse Lane, cross the Bentley Canal, then via a turntable to run into the manure and acid works of William Bradburn. Although so described, this works must actually have been an early chemical works, as the 'manure' was actually fertiliser and not a natural animal product. The works was situated on the southern side of the Wyrley & Essington Canal and on the western side of Backhouse Lane. The evidence of a turntable suggests that rail traffic was horse drawn from the exchange sidings into the works. However, by 1887 the turntable and line into these works had disappeared. Instead, the line was double for about 100 yards as it made the 90 degree turn northwards from its junction with the WWR line, suggesting that this was the exchange point for private traffic. After crossing the canal it then continued directly northwards squeezing between Backhouse Lane on the left and the Imperial Galvanised Iron Works to its right. The termination of this line

This interesting MR signal at Heath Town Junction survived until early 1960. The twin home arms served to distinguish between routes into the Wednesfield goods yard, and the connection to the former GWR line at Wolverhampton Low Level. The wooden signal post was topped with a decorative splined finial. The location was just next to the bridge over Inkerman Street, which can be seen in the foreground.
R.S. Carpenter Collection

A Midland Railway land boundary marker post still extant in the embankment at Heath Town around 1990.
S. Dewey

acted as a headshunt, and rail traffic would then have to reverse into the Imperial Galvanized Iron Works. Several lines are shown within this works, which expanded eastwards alongside the Bentley Canal over the years. The extent of the private railway system here suggests that horse power would not have been sufficient, but there is no alternative evidence to suggest that the MR and its successors performed whatever shunting was necessary. Nor is there any evidence that this firm owned its own locomotives.

By 1901 this works had disappeared, and the eastern half of the site was occupied by the chocolate and confectionery works of the Birmingham firm of Patterson & Gears at the junction of Hall Street and Well Lane. The aforementioned lines were all removed, and instead another turntable was installed on the line from the WWR near where the original turntable had been, but this time leading to a line in the opposite direction, alongside the confectionery works. These works were afterwards taken over by the Patent Axle Box Co. This line, or rather extended siding, seemed to remain *in situ* up to the time in 1936 when the works of Ductile Steel Co. were erected on the empty ground south of the Bentley Canal and on the left of the WWR as it approached Wednesfield. These works were served by a single siding on the formation of the original line mentioned above, and were normally shunted by the LMS, with internal movements performed by a road tractor until a locomotive was purchased in 1965 (*see Appendix One*). At this time further sidings were provided for the company. Rail traffic to this works eventually ceased around July 1981.

Wednesfield gets its name from the bloody battle of 'Wodensfield' which allegedly took place nearby at New Cross in 910 AD when the Saxons under the leadership of Edward the Elder beat the Danish Vikings. But more recently, at the opening of the WWR, the population of Wednesfield was around 9,000 although that increased most markedly after World War I when the area became something of an overspill development of housing for Wolverhampton, particularly to the north and east of the town. By 1965 the population was of the order of 35,000. Meanwhile, the metal working industries in the area had also developed considerably with such firms as Brockhouse Castings, C. & B. Smith, Jenks & Cattell, Richards & Ross, Willenhall Motor Radiator Co. and Weldless Steel Tube Co. becoming established especially in the area to the south of the station, along Neachells Lane. These firms undoubtedly contributed to the traffic passing through Wednesfield goods yard.

Neachells Lane crossed the railway at the eastern end of **Wednesfield** station (1¾ miles) and provided access to it and to the goods yard. The goods facilities were all on the northern (up) side of the line and comprised three sidings, one of which passed through the substantial wooden goods shed, which, attractively for a goods shed, featured a hipped roof. Two further short sidings were sited alongside the up platform, giving access to side- and end-loading platforms. Goods facilities were not provided from the 1872 opening of the line, but came into use in 1876, with further provision for minerals in the following year. The station buildings were located on the up platform and comprised two brick-built gable ended structures positioned side by side and at right angles to the line, the westernmost one being slightly smaller. Beyond these in the Walsall direction a range of three single-storey structures with tiled gable-ended roofs

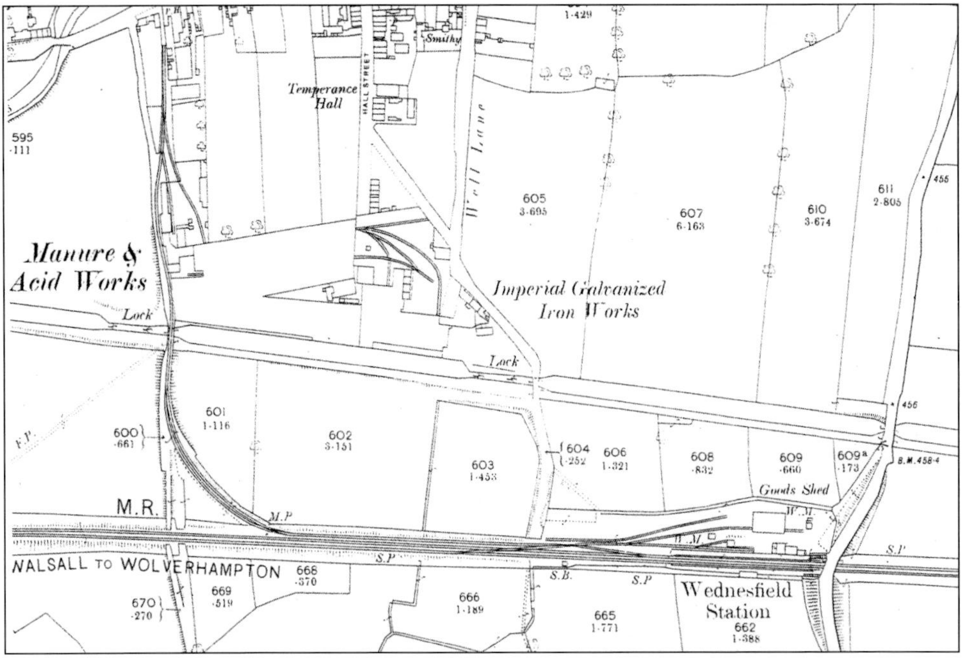

Wednesfield, showing the line serving local businesses in 1887. The tramway to Bradburn's Manure & Acid Works had been removed by this date and the line extended eastwards into the Imperial Galvanized Iron Works. *Reproduced from 25 in. Ordnance Survey map, 1887*

Wednesfield. By 1902 the iron works had gone, and the site used for Paterson & Gears' Chocolate & Confectionery Works. The lines were thus considerably simplified.
Reproduced from 25 in. Ordnance Survey map, 1902

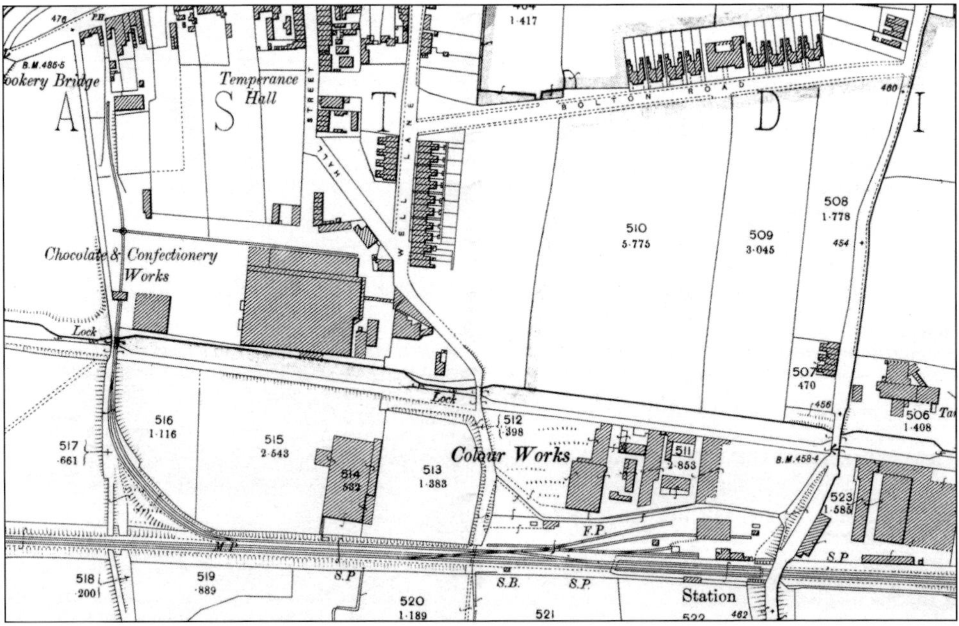

Wednesfield station around 1960, looking towards Wolverhampton. The station buildings appear to have been taken over by the engineering department, but the goods yard is still quite busy. Note the signal box in the centre left of the photograph. *D. Wilson*

Wednesfield station looking towards Walsall, taken from the leading auto coach of the SLS rail tour visiting Black Country lines on 26th May, 1951. The goods shed was still intact, if not in actual use, as were the station buildings. The large building looming behind the station was the entrance and offices of the edge making firm of Jenks & Cattell Co. Ltd on Neachells Lane.
R.S. Carpenter Collection

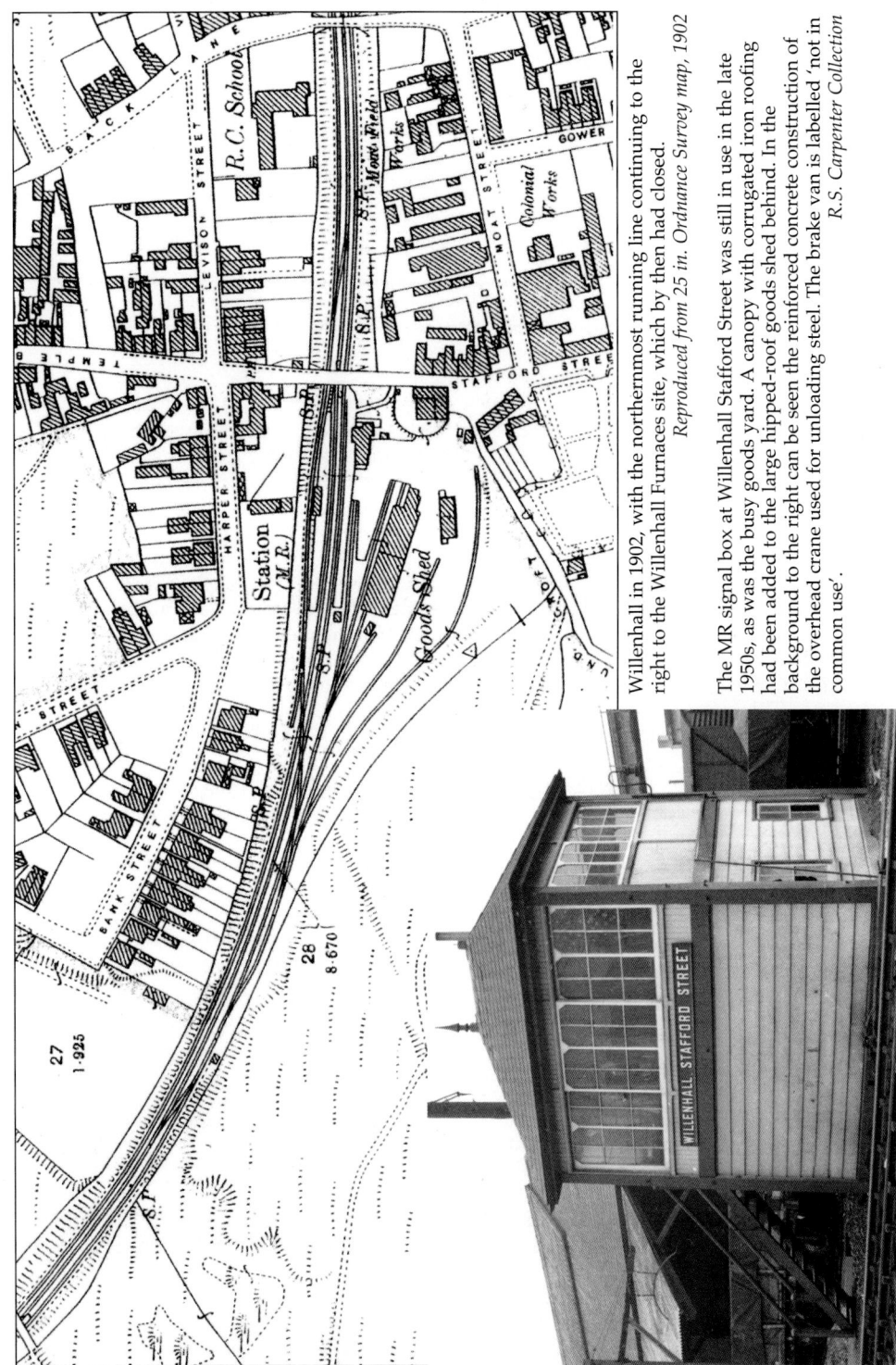

Willenhall in 1902, with the northernmost running line continuing to the right to the Willenhall Furnaces site, which by then had closed.
Reproduced from 25 in. Ordnance Survey map, 1902

The MR signal box at Willenhall Stafford Street was still in use in the late 1950s, as was the busy goods yard. A canopy with corrugated iron roofing had been added to the large hipped-roof goods shed behind. In the background to the right can be seen the reinforced concrete construction of the overhead crane used for unloading steel. The brake van is labelled 'not in common use'.
R.S. Carpenter Collection

were positioned parallel to the line, and abutting the main buildings. These three buildings gradually diminished in size as they progressed away from the main building - giving the impression that as time went on a smaller and smaller addition was made, although they are believed to have all actually been constructed at the same time. Somewhat oddly, there was a bay window projecting out from the first single-storey building on to the platform, presumably so that the station master could observe activity on the platform without going outside. In earlier days such features normally contained signalling apparatus before the introduction of signal boxes, so perhaps this was an architectural remnant from those times. The main buildings functioned primarily as the station master's house, whilst the booking hall, waiting rooms and staff rooms were located in the single-storey extension. A small waiting shelter was situated on the down platform, which was accessed by a flight of steps from the Neachells Lane overbridge. A similar flight of steps also led to the up platform, as an alternative to using the station forecourt. A signal box was situated on the down side just beyond the platform end, and conveniently opposite the goods sidings. The original signal box was replaced on 23rd October, 1898 by a standard MR hipped-roof structure which remained in use until 1st August, 1965. Station masters here were recorded in 1877 as being John Grundy (recalled by old inhabitants as 'a pleasant and helpful character'), in 1888 as being John Drummond and by 1924 as Walter Reginald Pumfrey.

Leaving Wednesfield, the line first crossed the short Neachell branch of the Bentley Canal, which served several small collieries to the south in the Neachell area. This short branch canal was of only 3 furlongs length and had opened in 1845. Meanwhile the main line of the Bentley Canal ran parallel a short distance to the north of the line. This had opened in 1843 running $3^3/_8$ miles from a junction with the Wyrley & Essington Canal at New Cross to a junction with the BCN Anson Branch at Bentley. Having been closed to commercial traffic in 1953, both the main line and the Neachell branch gradually became disused and were filled in during the early 1960s.

Next the line fell at 1 in 100 for a short distance, then reached an area of flat ground before it passed beneath Noose Lane, turned south-eastwards and entered a cutting on the outskirts of Willenhall. Near here, the line was crossed by the narrow gauge tramways of the Chillington Iron Co. Ltd running from their collieries in the area, and also those of the Willenhall Furnace Co. linking their collieries in the Sneyd and Little London areas to their iron works. Both eventually employed narrow gauge steam locomotives as replacements for horses on these tramways.

Willenhall (3 miles) was world famous for its lock-making industry, with such names as Squires, Yale and Union being the most prominent. Like most other towns in the area it also spawned numerous businesses engaged in metal working. The station (3 miles) was situated in a cutting, and comprised a single platform on the down side with the main station buildings, and an island platform on the up side. However, there was only one platform face on this island platform, the rear being secured by a wall, as the line behind it was effectively a goods loop. A waiting shelter was provided in the centre of this platform, which could only be accessed by way of a wooden barrow crossing from the down

A general view of the station at Willenhall Stafford Street in the late 1950s, looking towards Walsall. The platform and station building remain on the down side, although the up platform has been cleared. *R.S. Carpenter Collection*

Looking towards Wolverhampton from the signal box at Willenhall Stafford Street in the late 1950s. The connections for goods traffic to enter the yard from both directions are clearly evident. *R.S. Carpenter Collection*

platform. The station buildings were replicas of those at Wednesfield. A signal box was sited at the westernmost end of the down platform, and adjacent to the goods yard. The original box was replaced on 26th October, 1893 by a standard MR hipped-roof box, which continued in use until 1st August, 1965. The station was opened with the line as 'Willenhall Market Place', but was renamed simply Willenhall from 1st April, 1904, becoming Willenhall Stafford Street on 2nd June, 1924 under the LMS to distinguish it from its LNWR neighbour on the former GJR line. The goods yard was quite substantial, with a long headshunt running westwards from the down line parallel with the running tracks. From this, or via a crossover from the up line at the western end of the platform, the yard led to four sidings. One passed through a single-road wooden goods shed similar to the one at Wednesfield, whilst the remainder spanned out into the yard. A further siding was sited behind the down platform giving access to a side- and end-loading bay. In many ways the yard layout was similar to that at Wednesfield, but faced in the opposite direction. A later addition was a massive gantry crane spanning two of the tracks in the yard.

Willenhall was jocularly known as 'Humpshire' in the Midlands. This is attributed to the workers, stooping over their benches as they filed keys and assembled locks, who developed humps on their backs from this posture!

Leaving Willenhall, the line continued in a cutting with the goods loop running alongside for some distance, passing under Back Lane and a continuation of this loop forming a headshunt for a further distance. This was actually the remnants of a 600 yds-long line installed in 1877 to connect to the Willenhall Furnaces Co. Construction had been approved by the MR General Purposes Committee on 6th March, 1877 at an estimated cost of £750. This company acquired a locomotive to work this line, and details are given in *Appendix One*. It was therefore unfortunate that so soon after, this company succumbed during the severe recession affecting the iron and steel industry and closed on 9th April, 1881.

The line now proceeded north-eastwards, climbing first at 1 in 275, then 1 in 228 and out on to a small embankment, passing over Stringers Lane then the Bentley Canal before arriving at **Short Heath** station (3¾ miles). Various collieries littered the landscape here, as elsewhere earlier on the line, indicating the reason why so much heavy industry had settled in the area. The station here had opened with the line, being officially known as Short Heath (Clarke's Lane), but unofficially as one or the other. The 'e' in Clarke's Lane also appears to have been optional over the years. Again the station buildings were replicas of those at Wednesfield, but this time the main buildings were on the up platform, with the single-storey extensions running away to the east, complete with the bay window protrusion on to the platform. A fairly substantial wooden shelter was provided on the opposite platform, with access to be gained only by a boarded crossing from the up platform. However, it would appear that in later years unofficial paths from Clarke's Lane were worn into the embankment by the continued passage of feet seeking a short-cut. The line then passed over Clarke's Lane on a plate girder bridge, from which road a driveway led to the station forecourt on the up side. There was a single siding and a side- and end-loading dock on a further siding behind the up platform to cater for goods traffic which began in 1877. This was supplemented by the construction of Willenhall Gas Co.

Short Heath station, still remarkably intact, around 1960 and looking towards Walsall. The interesting feature here is that the platform height remains at a low level, as originally built. Undoubtedly, had the station not closed in 1931, the height would have been increased to the standard required by the LMSR. *D. Wilson*

An undated aerial view at Short Heath, looking north. Beyond the station are the works and sidings of the Willenhall Gas Company. *Author's Collection*

DESCRIPTION OF THE LINE

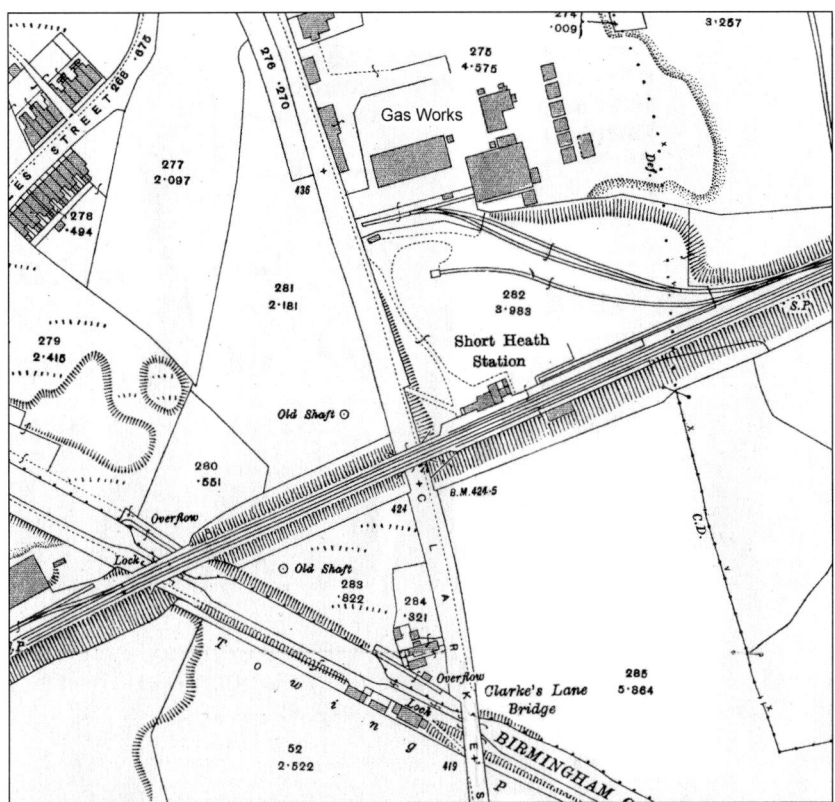

By 1902 the Willenhall Gas Works at Short Heath was in operation, served by two sidings for incoming coal and outgoing coke and other waste products.

Reproduced from 25 in. Ordnance Survey map, 1914

works on a site to the north of the goods yard around 1894 (replacing an earlier very much smaller works in Lower Lichfield Street, Willenhall). This was given two further sidings and a backshunt into the retort house. By the late 1930s the works were producing about 11,000 tons of coke annually, with up to 27,000 tons of coal delivered there for carbonizing, divided almost equally between coal from North Staffordshire, Yorkshire, North Wales and Derbyshire. Presumably local coal did not possess adequate properties for gas production. The Willenhall Gas Co. actually owned its own fleet of wagons, numbering around 50 in the 1920s. As there was only a trailing connection from the up line to the yard, all full and empty coal trains could only enter the yard from this direction. The works continued in production up to the mid-1950s. Even though Short Heath was never a block post it was provided with a signal box, but this did not open until 17th November, 1903.

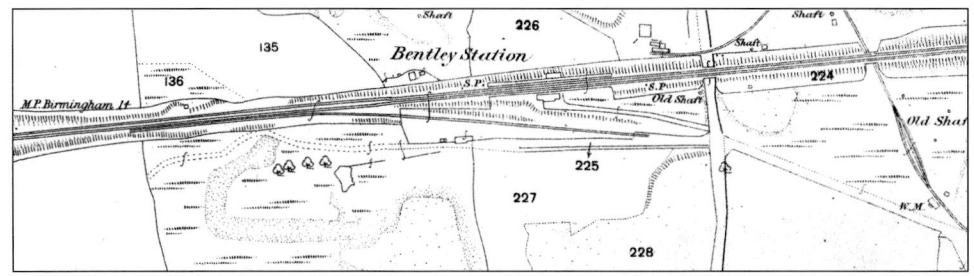

Bentley station was short lived, closing in 1898, and was served by just one siding for goods traffic.
Reproduced from 25 in. Ordnance Survey map, 1886

View along the WWR route from near Bentley, looking westwards toward Willenhall.
R. Selvey Collection

An ex-LMS Fowler '4F' class 0-6-0 approaches Bentley with a short freight in the early 1960s. The track had recently been reballasted - almost guaranteeing that the line would be closed shortly!
R. Selvey Collection

Continuing eastwards the line passed through a wooded and fairly rural landscape rising at 1 in 140 for ½ mile before reaching a summit and descending at 1 in 200, crossing the Bentley Canal and arriving at **Bentley** station (4¾ miles). Nothing much is known of this station building, which was located on the down side, as no details or photographs of it have been traced. It had opened with the line, but was not a block post, although it was provided with a signal box before August 1877 and probably closed at the same time as the station, but in any event by May 1899. It is interesting to note that on 19th July, 1883 the MR Way & Works Committee approved a minute from the Traffic Committee dated 14th March that year 'agreeing to pay Lord Lichfield £1,000 for a bridge agreed to be built at 4 miles 28 chains on the Wolverhampton & Walsall branch, and also as to keeping open Bentley station for three years'. The bridge must have been nearby here, and Lord Lichfield had, of course, been the Chairman of the WWR – but there was evidently some concern about the viability of this station. In fact, a further agreement at this time was that the Earl of Lichfield would pay for any deficit arising between the receipts and the costs of maintaining the station. By 1895, the expenses totalled £426 whilst the receipts were just £12 ! Evidently, the Earl was not prepared to continue with his subsidy indefinitely, and it was closed on 1st October, 1898 to passengers and goods. It is not known when Bentley station was demolished, but this is surely likely to have occurred by the early part of the 20th century.

Leaving Bentley station, the line crossed Bloxwich Lane and continued to fall at 1 in 200 on an embankment through an area once again littered with coal mines. It crossed another tramway of the Chillington Iron Co. Ltd linking furnaces and coal mines in this area with a connection to the BCN Anson Branch Canal, which was mostly out of use by 1884. Soon afterwards the line crossed this canal, alongside which the BCN had also constructed its own Hatherton Tramway linking some of Lord Hatherton's mines in the area to the canal - but this too was disused by the 1870s. The number of small coal and limestone mines in this area declined rapidly in the second half of the 19th century, so that there were no coal mines by 1882, and limestone working had ceased within another 10 years.

Jack Haddock recalls that near here a tramp took up residence in a disused platelayer's hut (the type made from old sleepers and painted black). He became known for his flock of chickens that foraged alongside the running line. In the winter, well meaning engine crews would often drop a lump of coal for him as they passed.

About ¼ mile further on the line entered a cutting, but just before was a group of three double-ended sidings on the northern side. From the western end of these a separate line headed north to a processing plant which recovered usable material from the many slag heaps and spoil mines in the immediate area (notably those of Phillip William's Old Birchills Furnace) to create fertilizer and road-making material. A further connection led to the Green Lane Furnaces of Birchills Furnaces Ltd opening around 1911 and featuring a triangular junction in its formation. A signal box (Birchills Sidings) was installed on the southern side of the line, opposite this connection and associated sidings to control access here, opening on 19th January, 1911.These furnaces and this connection continued in operation until around 1932. The locomotives used on this system from its connection with the WWR are also given in *Appendix One*. During the 1930s the former colliery and furnace sites were designated as landfill sites, and waste material from all over the West Midlands tipped their loads here. This wagon load material was assembled at the MR goods yard in Tasker Street, Walsall and a trip working run 'as required' to the sidings. The sidings were revised over the years to adapt to their new role, so that in its later years the box was remarked to have 45 levers, of which 36 were painted white to indicate that they were not in use! This box was eventually replaced by the one mentioned below, although it must have seen little use for many years. Due to its somewhat remote location, the nearest supply of drinking water was the Victory Inn. It is remarked that as the box was not very busy throughout the day, when the signalman went to the inn, he collected more than just his water. In fact, in later years the box was not continually manned - so that when a spoil train was due, the signalman at North Walsall would close his box and join the train. Once at Birchills sidings, he would open the box and control the shunting movements. When complete, he would join the return working and alight at North Walsall, where he would reopen his box.

The sidings on the northern side of the line were completely relaid around 1948 in connection with the building of the new power station (see next paragraph) and the connection to Green Lane Furnaces was removed. A single extension siding at the eastern end of this group was made, so that waste material could be unloaded and taken to landfill sites further north-eastward than those mentioned above. A signal box named Birchills Power Station Sidings was installed in the centre of these northern sidings, almost opposite the original signal box, which it replaced, coming into use on 20th November, 1949.

Almost opposite this point, and on the south side of the line, was the connection to Birchills power station, which had been erected by Walsall Corporation and opened on 31st October, 1916. Lying alongside the Birchills branch of the Wyrley & Essington Canal it initially relied on coal from the Cannock Chase collieries delivered entirely by canal. It passed to the West Midlands Joint Electricity Authority in 1927, and a new power station was erected alongside the existing station at around the same time as it was nationalized, on 1st April, 1948 as part of the British Electricity Authority. This in turn became the Central Electricity Authority from 1st April, 1955, then the Central Electricity Generating Board from 1st January, 1958. The new station was commissioned on 30th September, 1949, and was distinguished by its six cooling towers. In that same year extensive sidings were put in on the south side of the line and the connection made to the WWR. These sidings were later extended westwards (still on the south side of the line) beyond the former BCN Anson Branch Canal, and almost to the site of the original station at Bentley. Deliveries by rail to the power station commenced soon after, but with the gradual demise of coal working on Cannock Chase during the 1960s the power station had to rely on sources from further afield. It operated several locomotives, details of which are to be found in *Appendix One*. With the closure of the WWR line westwards in 1965, the Birchills Power Station Sidings signal box was downgraded, and replaced by a ground frame from 4th June, 1967. However, rail traffic ceased in 1978 after which the power station was decommissioned in October 1982 and the track removed. In fact, the last train to leave Birchills power station sidings was on 5th December, 1978 (reporting No. 8T34, part of Bescot Target 45 working).The power station was finally demolished in March 1987. Some of the main line workings here will be found in Chapter Six.

Shortly afterwards the line passed beneath the Birchills Branch Canal, then almost immediately beneath Green Lane (now the A34) falling at 1 in 100 for almost ½ mile. The line continued in the cutting at its approach to **North Walsall** station (6 miles). This station was a typical suburban station with no goods facilities and being located in a cutting, access to the two side platforms was from the Bloxwich Road bridge (now B4210) crossing the line at its eastern end. Booking offices, waiting rooms, lavatories and staff offices were executed mostly in brick and located on each platform. Due to its closeness to Walsall, and competition from trams and later buses on the neighbouring main road this station soon succumbed, and closed as from 13th July, 1925. However, it was not demolished right away, as during the 1930s it was reopened on more than one occasion for special trips run for local inhabitants. One such was a trip organized by the nearby St Peter's church for a day out at Sutton Park. The train for this excursion had originated in Wolverhampton, and used the direct line to Lichfield Road Junction. On the far side of the road bridge a signal box was situated in the embankment on the north side of the line, to control the junction of the direct line to Water Orton and the line into Walsall. This box was opened in 1879 with the WWMJR line, was reframed by 31st May, 1896 and replaced by a standard MR hipped-roof box on 28th October 1906, finally closing on 4th June, 1967 a month after the direct line was officially closed (*see below*).

The direct line continued more or less eastwards soon being elevated on an embankment to gain height, passing beneath Coal Pool Lane and crossing the LNWR (SSR) Cannock line on a plate girder bridge. As it neared the southern boundary of Ryecroft cemetery it passed over Mill Lane, then on the left could be seen the earthworks of the connection to the LNWR (SSR) Lichfield line that was never laid with track, as mentioned in Chapter Two. The Lichfield line was crossed on another plate girder bridge and the line reached Lichfield Road Junction just at the point at which Cartbridge Lane passes beneath in a narrow brick-built bridge. The distance between North Walsall Junction signal box and that at Lichfield Road Junction was 1,417 yards (0.8 mile) on a gradient of 1 in 100 falling from North Walsall.

This direct line found alternative uses in the 1930s, when for example, the Bertram Mills Circus performed at Walsall Arboretum. On more than one occasion, the circus train empty stock was stabled on the direct line for several days. Similarly, during the coal strike of 1932, surplus coal wagons were stored here. Local lads (Jack Haddock amongst them) would surreptitiously remove small amounts of grease from the axle boxes, which proved to be an excellent shoe polish !

Reverting to North Walsall, the Walsall line turned south-eastwards and began to descend at 1 in 100 in a deep cutting between rows of houses and various industrial premises, and by the time it had passed beneath Mill Street was then facing directly southwards. A 45 mph speed restriction applied on this

North Walsall Junction facing east, with the original WWR line to Walsall disappearing to the right beyond the road overbridge. The WWMJR direct line to Lichfield Road Junction and Water Orton proceeds straight on, albeit with a double curvature in the line, presumably necessary to line up at the junction. The vantage point for this undated photo is the site of the North Walsall station, long since demolished. The advertising hoardings display the attractions of Walsall Fair, although the dates cannot be read.

Author's Collection

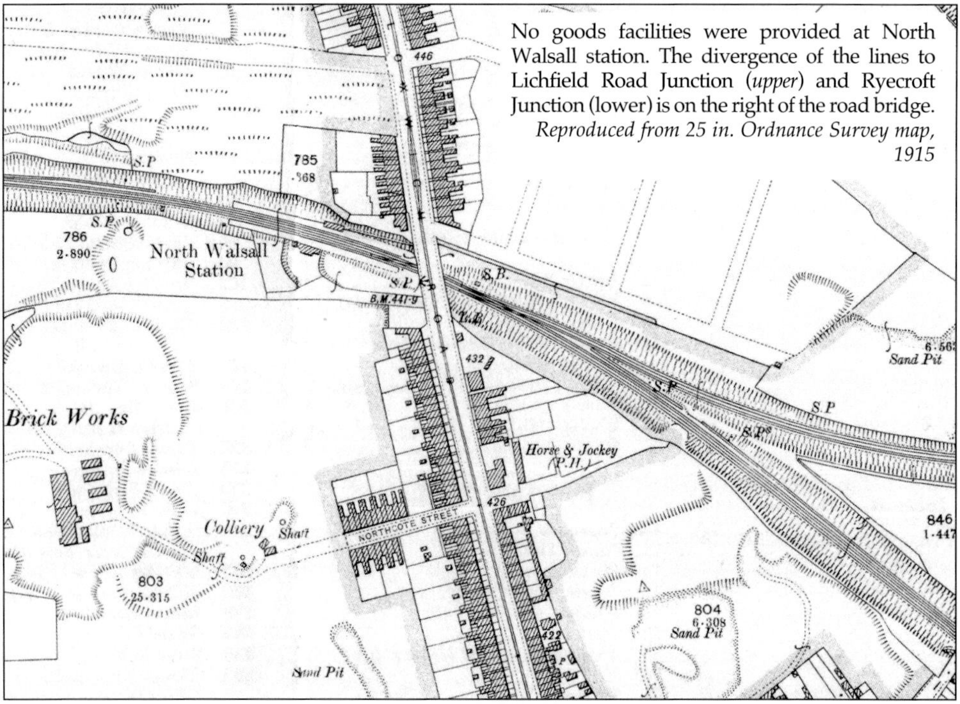

No goods facilities were provided at North Walsall station. The divergence of the lines to Lichfield Road Junction (*upper*) and Ryecroft Junction (lower) is on the right of the road bridge.

Reproduced from 25 in. Ordnance Survey map, 1915

North Walsall Junction looking towards Wolverhampton, with the hipped-roof MR signal box on the right. The junction for the Walsall line is to the left, and the direct route towards Water Orton to the right, in the foreground. The station, closed on 13th July, 1925 was located just beyond the overbridge which carried the Bloxwich Road, but all traces had gone by the time this photograph was taken on 3rd October, 1965. *J. Alsop/Kidderminster Railway Museum*

In the mid-1960s, two Stanier '8F' class 2-8-0s are seen battling towards North Walsall Junction with a coal train from the Cannock Chase collieries which had reversed near to Walsall station. Two engines were required for the heavy workings to Birchills power station. The signal box controlling this junction can be seen in the distance, just before the road overbridge.
R. Selvey Collection

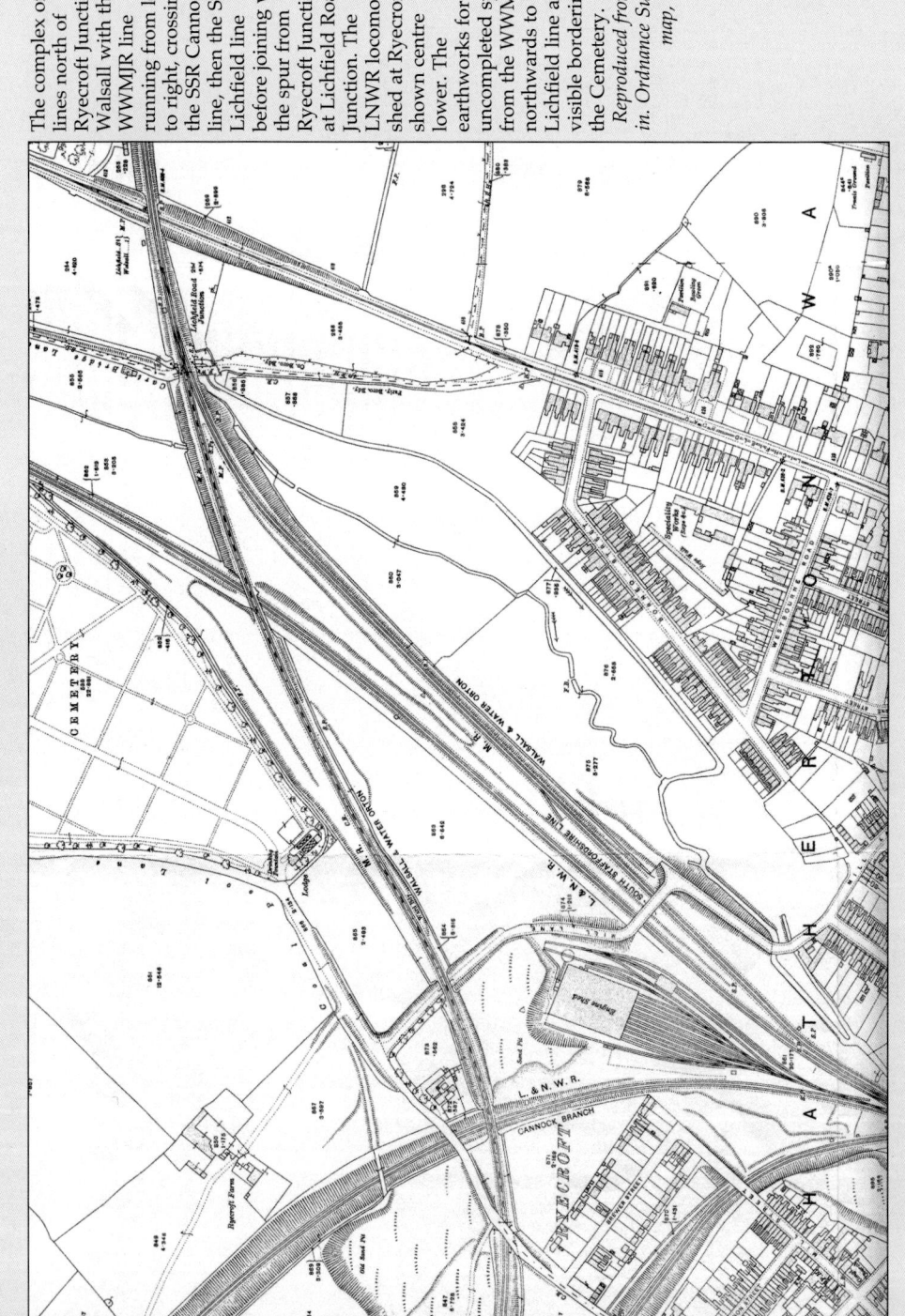

The complex of lines north of Ryecroft Junction, Walsall with the WWMJR line running from left to right, crossing the SSR Cannock line, then the SSR Lichfield line before joining with the spur from Ryecroft Junction at Lichfield Road Junction. The LNWR locomotive shed at Ryecroft is shown centre lower. The earthworks for the uncompleted spur from the WWMJR northwards to the Lichfield line are visible bordering the Cemetery.
Reproduced from 25 in. Ordnance Survey map, 1914

section, although that never likely to be exceeded by coal trains heading up the grade. It joined the LNWR lines at Ryecroft Jn just south of the junction of the Cannock and Lichfield lines, and then proceeded on LNWR tracks into Walsall station. At the time of opening in 1872 this approach to Walsall was a simple double track affair, but it was widened in 1879-83 into four tracks, eliminating a considerable bottleneck.

Starting the next leg of our journey at Ryecroft Junction, the WWMJR diverged from the LNWR Lichfield line just north of the Cannock line junction, and almost opposite the later junction for the 1880 locomotive shed at Ryecroft. The double track line was subject to a 60 mph limit and climbed north-eastwards at 1 in 100 on an embankment to Lichfield Road Junction and was controlled by a signal box (Ryecroft Junction) sited on the north side of the line, east of the junction and opened on 19th May, 1879. This box was replaced by one of the ubiquitous MR hipped boxes on 1st July, 1900 and finally closed on 4th June, 1967. Traffic ceased over the direct line between Lichfield Road Junction and North Walsall Junction as from 7th June, 1965, the line was taken out of use on 30th April, 1967 and officially closed the following day. The line from Ryecroft was hit by an enemy bomb during World War II, and although the track was repaired and returned to use speedily, for many years engine crews could always tell the spot, because there was a distinctly different sound as the wheels passed over it.

Now the line proceeds directly eastwards on an embankment, crossing the Lichfield Road (now A461) on another tall single-arch blue-brick bridge, and reaching some fairly open countryside. After ¾ mile, a trailing connection was made into the double sidings of a lime works. This access was only available from the eastbound line, and was controlled by a ground frame, the key for which was kept at the Lichfield Road Junction signal box. The main line companies performed all shunting duties here, for which no opening or closing dates have been traced.

From this point, the line enters a cutting, and just under a ¼ mile later, passes beneath the single-arch blue-brick-built aqueduct which carries both the BCN Daw End Branch Canal that caused considerable problems during its construction, and a lane which is a continuation of Park Road. Continuing in this cutting it passes beneath Bosty Lane (B4154) carried on a lofty three-arch blue-brick bridge and approaches **Aldridge** (9 miles), which is the summit of the climb for the last two miles, initially at 1 in 176 then 1 in 100. Five sidings were provided on the north side of the eastbound line, immediately before the line to Brownhills swung in on the left, and were accessed by a trailing junction. The three northernmost were single-ended: the first two were about 170 yards long, and the third (centre in this group) was 300 yards long terminating just before the Dumble Derry Lane road overbridge. The final pair (alongside the up running line) were double-ended, with the pointwork just to the east of the road bridge. A refuge siding at the exit of this group of sidings protected movements on the main line. The small goods yard could only be accessed from the Brownhills branch. The brick-built single-road goods shed had a hipped and slated roof and two delivery platforms for road vehicles surmounted with individual wooden cantilevered canopies. A further siding was positioned alongside, then a group of two at the far side of an extensive yard area. These

Ryecroft shed, Walsall after its rebuilding by BR with a new roof and other modernizations. This view is taken in the mid-1950s and features Stanier class '4' 2-6-4Ts, Nos. 42570 and 42627, plus the rear of a Bowen-Cooke 0-8-0. *R.K. Blenkowe*

Bowen-Cooke 0-8-0 No. 49430 storms up the grade out of Walsall in 1964 on the spur from Ryecroft to North Walsall with a freight for the Wolverhampton direction. This section of line ran mostly in deep cuttings and was graded severely. *Transport Treasury/D. Durrant*

Former LNWR Bowen-Cooke 0-8-0 No. 49081 crosses Mill Lane bridge with a westbound freight working in the early 1960s. It is traversing the direct line between Lichfield Road Junction and North Walsall Junction. *R. Selvey Collection*

A former LNWR '7F' class 0-8-0 approaches Coal Pool Lane with a fairly lengthy coal train from the Water Orton direction, almost certainly bound for Birchills power station. It is on the WWMJR direct line from Lichfield Road Junction, and has just passed over the SSR Cannock line, the bridge abutments for which can be seen just beyond the new ballast on the right of the line. *R. Selvey Collection*

One of Mr Bowen-Cooke's celebrated '7F' 0-8-0s, No. 48895 running light engine from North Walsall to Lichfield Road Junction, near Proffitt Street. As will be apparent, this section of the direct line became increasingly unkempt as its impending closure loomed. *R. Selvey Collection*

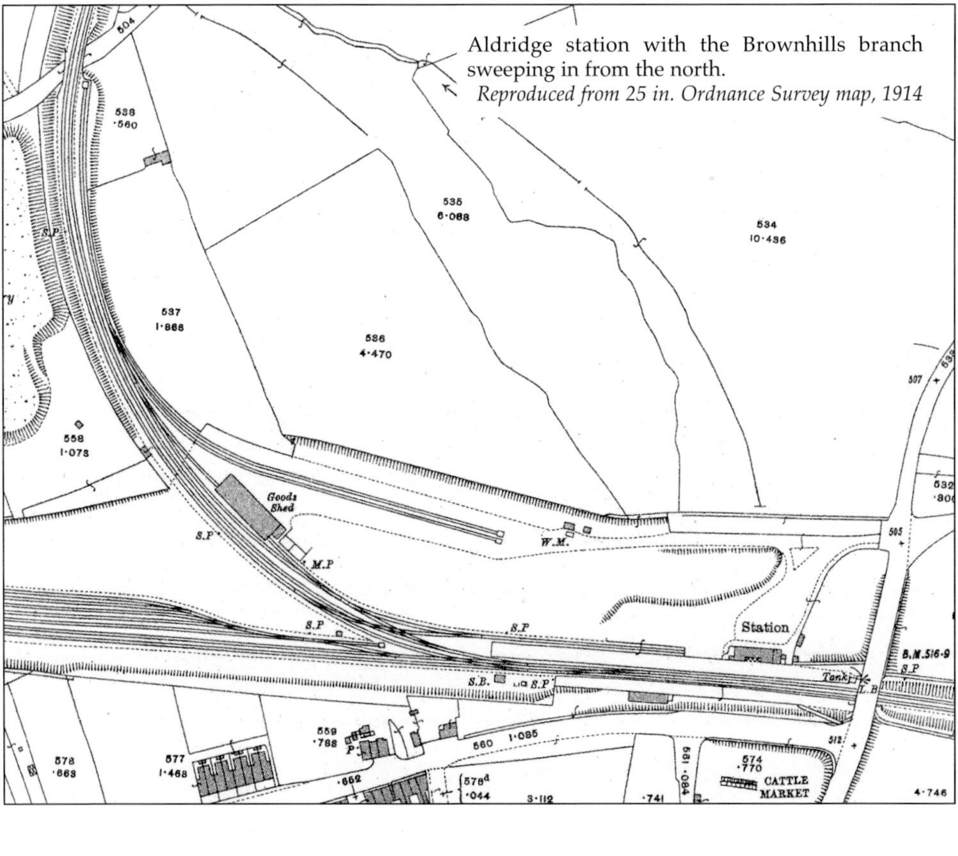

Aldridge station with the Brownhills branch sweeping in from the north.
Reproduced from 25 in. Ordnance Survey map, 1914

A postcard view of the main station buildings at Aldridge during the 1930s. The goods yard in the background seems to be particularly busy, with a collection of coal wagons, and various other vans and wagons containing a selection of goods. *Author's Collection*

A close view of the main station building, on the up platform at Aldridge, in 1956. Although many passengers are in evidence, no-one is taking advantage of the antique cast-iron personal weighing machine in the foreground. These were once a familiar sight at most stations.

D. Ibbotson

Streetly station around 1913 looking towards Walsall. The outer face of the island platform was still in use at that time, as was the signal box which closed and was removed in 1925. *L&GRP*

No goods facilities were provided at Streetly station. The line running behind the down platform was disused from around 1925 until reopened temporarily for the Scout Jamboree in 1957.

Reproduced from 25 in. Ordnance Survey map, 1924

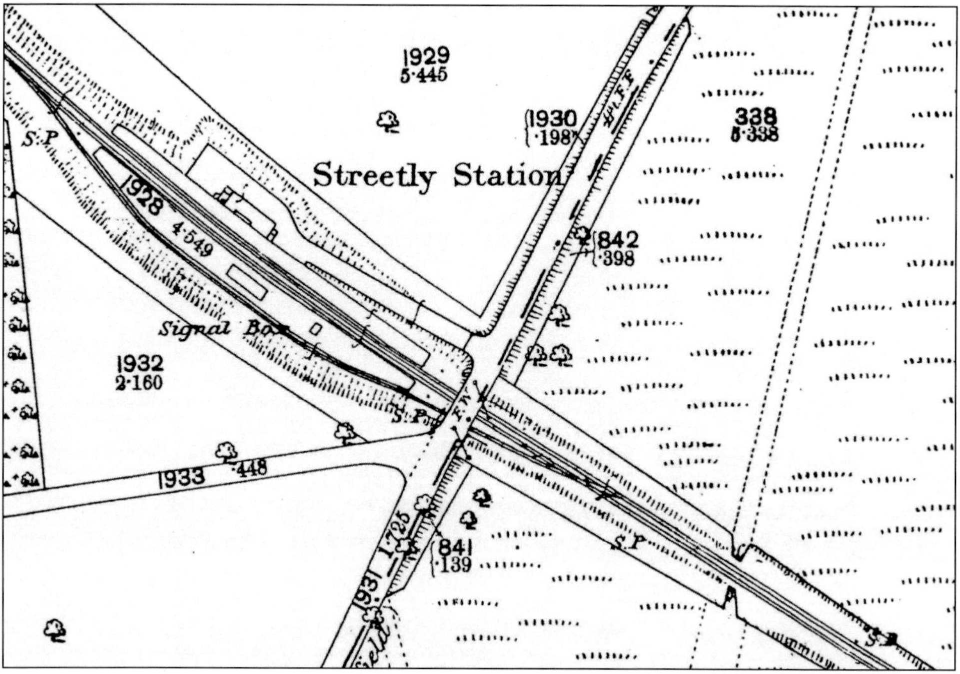

two sidings were used for coal traffic, so that coal dust created when the local coal merchants unloaded the wagons would not unduly affect passengers at the station. A weighbridge, with its obligatory office, was situated nearby. This area seemed as though it was destined to be filled in with more sidings, but was always left vacant and spacious. A further siding was provided at the rear of the eastbound platform, for the usual purposes of side- and end-loading of wagons and vans. This was only partially fenced off from the main platform, so that it could also be used for passenger trains on the Brownhills branch.

The station buildings were on the eastbound platform and reflected standard MR architecture of the time, a pleasing arrangement of two two-storey gable-ended buildings, end-on to the platform, with a single-storey structure linking them, but set back and with the same roof line. The space left by being set back was filled in with a glass canopy. So this arrangement provided the booking office, parcels office, waiting rooms, and a covered outside waiting area and became almost a standard design for MR stations. Various small brick-built flat-roofed buildings were sited at each end of this main structure for staff offices, toilets and stores. The platforms were both notably wide here, and both rear edges were finished with the distinctive MR diagonal wooden fencing. A fairly spacious brick-built waiting room was provided on the westbound platform. The signal box, of the usual MR hipped-roof design was positioned on the south side of the line, directly opposite the Brownhills line junction, and was a replacement on 3rd May, 1919 for the original box that opened with the line. In turn this one closed as from 18th May, 1969. Passenger access was via the station forecourt, and due to the lack of a footbridge, also by way of short steps from the Walsall Road (A454) overbridge at the eastern end of the station.

East of the station, the line passes into a cutting then out on to an embankment, falling at 1 in 100 and just as it passes over the Chester Road (A452) turns to the south, starts to climb now at 1 in 118 and passes once more into pleasant countryside, turning more to the east as it approaches **Streetly** station (11¾ miles) in a shallow cutting. The station was sited at the junction of Thornhill Road and Foley Road East, on the western boundary of Sutton Park. Although not provided with any goods facilities, the station did boast an island platform on the westbound side, thus giving three platform faces. A fairly small waiting room was sited here, along with a small signal box, rather unusually in the centre of the platform, and of the familiar MR hipped-roof design. As Streetly was not a block post, the signal box probably only functioned as weather protection for a lever frame. However, this box closed as from 26th October, 1925 and was removed some time later. Consequently, the outer platform face was rarely used, and was allowed to become overgrown, until the occasion of the Jamboree held at Sutton Park in 1957, for which the line was relaid. To permit use of this platform, a temporary block post was set up on the platform from 21st May, 1957. Contemporary photos show that this line did continue in use, even if only for storing wagons, at least for one more year. The main station buildings were on the eastbound platform, being almost identical to those at Aldridge. The station had originally opened with the line as 'Jervis Town', being named after the local landowner, Viscount St Vincent otherwise Edwin Swinfen Jervis, but within a matter of months was renamed 'Streetly'.

A late, similar view of Streetly station, taken some time in the 1930s, by which time the loop line and signal box had been removed. *Lens of Sutton/R.S. Carpenter*

Streetly station on 1st May, 1949 with Fowler '4F' class 0-6-0 No. 44069 on a lengthy permanent way train. Resleepering has evidently been going on, judging from the sleepers on the platform, and the lack of ballast on the up line. The engineers' mess coach behind the brake van seems to be of considerable vintage. *HMRS/ESR*

DESCRIPTION OF THE LINE

This view of Streetly station in the 1970s shows the station following closure. By this time it was truly abandoned, with vastly encroaching lineside foliage, but had thus far survived demolition. *Stations UK*

The line now enters Sutton Park and continues in a straight line south-eastwards, running in a cutting bordered by trees for most of its length and falling at a constant 1 in 165, passing Bracebridge Pool on the left and Blackroot Pool on the right. Eventually it emerges near to Sutton Coldfield and the next station **Sutton Park** (13¾ miles). This was situated some distance from the centre of Sutton Coldfield and its existence was primarily to serve visitors to Sutton Park. Consequently, several trains (from both directions) terminated here, especially excursions at summer weekends, and so a crossover was provided at the station for engines to change direction, as well as giving eastbound goods trains access to the goods yard. Once more an island platform was provided, but this time on the eastbound line, and was provided with a substantial waiting room in red brick (almost as large as the main station building), which was surmounted with a cast-iron water tank at the eastern end. The northern face of this island platform was taken out of use on 1st February, 1965, and the line removed. The main station buildings were once more replicas of the Aldridge buildings and were on the westbound platform at the end of a short driveway from Clifton Road. This station enjoyed a footbridge, which not only connected the two platforms, but was extended to the north to reach a footpath that led to Sutton Park. Its construction was of lattice ironwork. A signal box was sited just beyond the western end of the westbound platform, and replaced on 9th January, 1896 by the familiar MR hipped-roof box, which lasted until 10th August, 1969. Beyond the station and signal box, a double track loop led from the westbound line, one of which tracks passed through a single-road brick-built goods shed with hipped and slated roof, also as at Aldridge. This loop continued to a headshunt, from which reversal led to a two-road coal siding on the southern extremity of the goods yard. Once again, the goods yard was laid out in a spacious manner.

A study of Sutton Park station buildings on the down side platform around 1950. Tidiness is the order of the day, but it may be noticed that gas lamps still provided the only illumination on the platforms. *HMRS/REL*

Sutton Park was well provided with both goods and passenger facilities.
Reproduced from 25 in. Ordnance Survey map, 1887

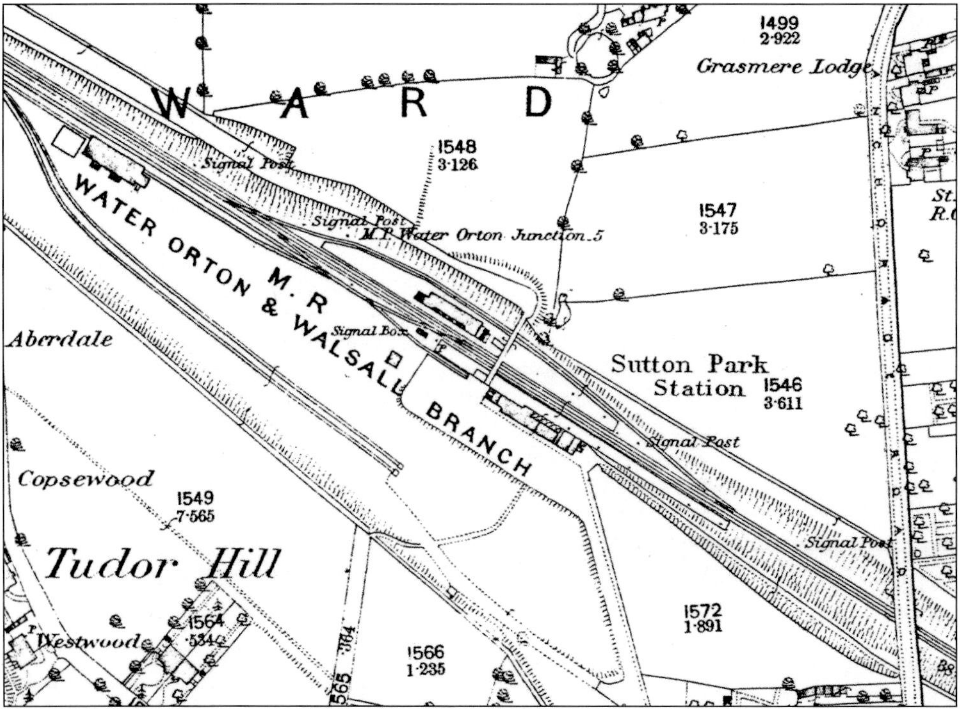

A roadside view of the station buildings at Sutton Park around 1950. A Scammell four-wheeled tractor unit with trailer awaits its next delivery. *HMRS/REL*

Sutton Park station on a sunny 15th September, 1955 looking towards Walsall, with a 'Super D' 0-8-0 lurking in the goods bay on the right. Almost alongside the goods shed a Metro-Cammell dmu is stationary on the running line to Walsall, with a group of men standing in front of it. Perhaps this was a test run, the unit has broken down? Would the 'Super D' provide assistance?
R.K. Blenkowe

The MR goods shed at Sutton Park had passed into the hands of the Post Office, but in this view from July 2008 was no longer in use. Nevertheless it was still quite complete, even down to the two wooden roadside canopies. *Author*

Sutton Town was a simple two platform passenger station. The LNWR line from Aston to Lichfield burrows beneath the WWMJR line, to the left of the station.

Reproduced from 25 in. Ordnance Survey map, 1887

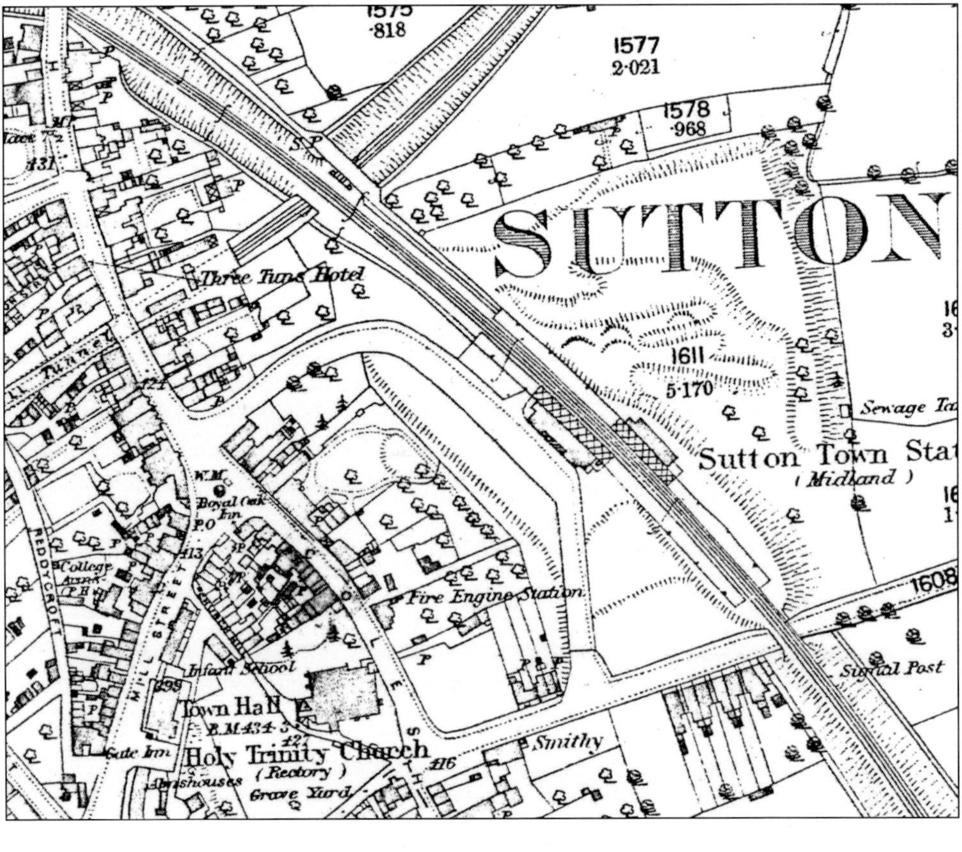

The spacious nature of the yard made it an attractive proposition for the establishment of a Forces Post Office during the early part of World War II, and this was duly constructed on the site of the former yard and coal depot, ironically using captured German prisoners of war as building labour. The building was served by a siding leading from the group of goods yard sidings. Around 1942/43 the US Army (Postal Force) took over the buildings to deal with letters and parcels for their forces in Europe. Local civilians were drafted in to assist, as well as staff members from the Birmingham Road post office. After the cessation of hostilities, the British Army Post Office took over until 1948 when it reverted to Post Office use, but specifically for British Commonwealth, foreign and forces parcels. After 1954 the use was that of a foreign post office for the exchange of letters, incoming and outgoing from all destinations abroad. Therefore, it will be appreciated that mail trains, and particularly parcels trains were a regular sight here during this period, but these ceased during 1987. Whilst this location still serves as a mail sorting depot, all deliveries are now made by road.

Sutton Park also served its country in a military manner. In the 19th century army volunteer camps were established at the Streetly end of the park, and during World War I the Birmingham City Battalion of the Royal Warwickshire Regiment trained at the park. During World War II further troops trained here, and tanks manufactured in the Black Country were tested here.

A quarter of a mile further on, having crossed the LNWR Aston to Lichfield line, was the station of **Sutton Town** (14 miles), situated to be more convenient to the centre of the prosperous town of Sutton Coldfield. It was opened with the line in 1879 as Sutton Coldfield, becoming Sutton Coldfield Town on 1st May, 1882, and reverting to plain Sutton Coldfield on 1st April, 1904. After the Grouping, it was renamed Sutton Town on 2nd June, 1924 by the LMS to distinguish it from its former LNWR neighbour, but only seven months later was closed as from 1st January, 1925. Under the LMS passengers were encouraged to use the LNWR line and station, and despite a petition presented by the town clerk containing 566 signatures the closure went ahead. This station building was the standard MR design as described for Aldridge, with the main station buildings on the westbound platform and quite a substantial waiting shelter on the eastbound platform. Unusually both buildings featured a full length glass canopy extending for the whole length of each of the buildings. Inconveniently, no footbridge was ever supplied, so the only pedestrian access to the eastbound platform was by a boarded crossing. A small signal box was apparently in use here for a very limited period of just one week, from 19th June until 26th June, 1898.

Passing over Coleshill Road the line continues on an embankment southwards, passing the rural New Hall Valley (New Hall Valley Country Park since 2005) on the left, crossing Plants Brook on an interesting small bridge. This is of blue brick construction, slightly skewed, and of two arches: one is quite large for the brook to flow through, and the other is much smaller and rounder to cater for the footpath, which was probably originally a small lane. The line then enters a cutting, falling all the time (1 in 100 for a mile, then 1 in 150 and 1 in 1320 for a further mile), at the approach to **Penns** station (16½ miles). This was renamed as 'Penns for Walmley' (Walmley is actually where the station is

Deeley MR 0-6-4T No. 2038 calls at Sutton Town station with a working from Birmingham New Street to Wolverhampton. Although the advertising hoarding declares 'Midland Railway', the locomotive bears its LMSR number and is in fully lined out red passenger livery. This dates the occasion to some time shortly after the Grouping, probably around 1925 or 1926. This also gives a rare view of the rail side of the station at Sutton Town. *R.S. Carpenter Collection*

The former MR station at Sutton Town has survived almost entirely completely, as seen here in July 2008. It is now in commercial use. *Author*

situated) on 17th October, 1936. Again the station was furnished with some sort of signal box for the same week in 1898 as Sutton Town station, but thereafter signalling arrangements were controlled at Penns Goods signal box (*see below*). The main station building was situated on the eastbound line, with the station forecourt connected to Penns Lane, from where a pedestrian footpath also led to the westbound platform. Station buildings followed the typical MR pattern.

The line continues south-easterly in a cutting to the site of Penns Goods Depot, where a goods yard was provided on the southern side of the westbound line, accessed from a headshunt which led by reversal to a loop line, one of which lines passed through the typical MR single-road hipped-roof goods shed. By a further reversal this gave access to two more goods sidings, one of which was furnished with cattle pens. The signal box was located on the north side of the line opposite the goods depot, and the original box was reframed on 7th June, 1896. It closed on 7th May, 1922 after which the goods lines were controlled by a ground frame, although this was upgraded to a block post during the Jamboree from 21st May, 1957, in order to increase line capacity.

As the line nears its end it falls constantly, first at 1 in 180 then more steeply at 1 in 104, and continues on an embankment into Minworth, crossing the Fazeley Canal and the main Birmingham to Lichfield Road (A38) much rebuilt and expanded in recent years. Immediately after crossing Park Lane it reaches (not surprisingly) Park Lane Junction (17½ miles), where the route diverges to

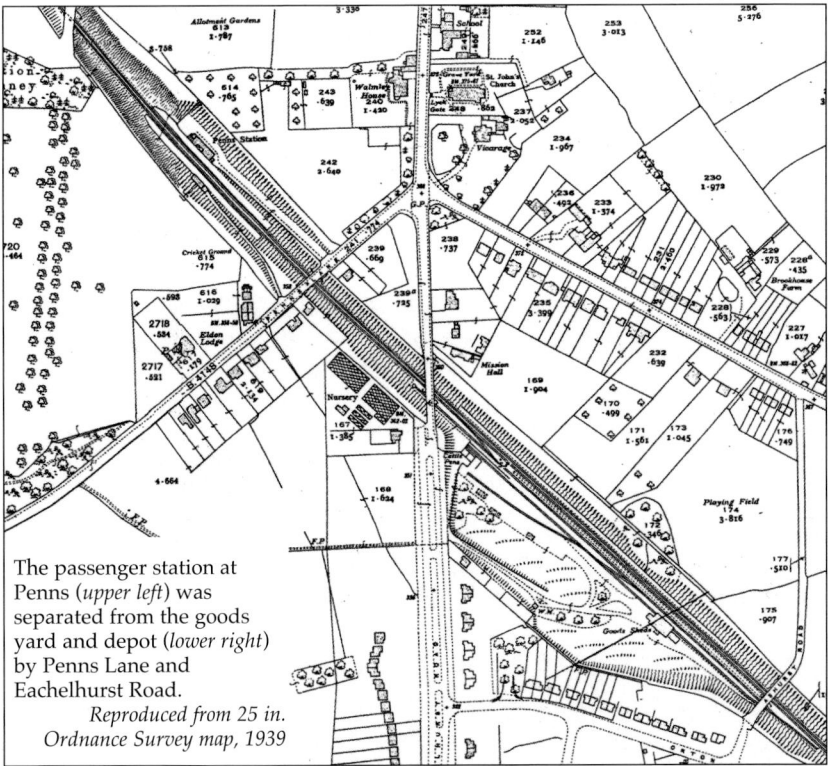

The passenger station at Penns (*upper left*) was separated from the goods yard and depot (*lower right*) by Penns Lane and Eachelhurst Road.
Reproduced from 25 in. Ordnance Survey map, 1939

Penns station looking west around 1912. The substantial brick structures on both platforms are complemented by profuse flower beds. The boarded crossing in the foreground formed the only means of transfer from one platform to the other without having to use the road bridge from which the photograph was taken. *Lens of Sutton Association*

Penns station in the 1930s appearing little changed from the 1912 view. Although taken on a rather gloomy day, the platforms, buildings and flower beds are still well cared for, as is the permanent way. *Lens of Sutton Association*

Penns station was built to the pleasing standard MR design of the time, neatly executed in red brick, and flanked by the traditional MR diagonal wooden fencing. Fowler class '4' 2-6-4T No. 42337 arrives at Penns on 20th June, 1949 with a service for Walsall. *HMRS/ESR*

Park Lane Junction and the chords leading south-east to Water Orton and south-west to Castle Bromwich are difficult to photograph, as the lines run on embankments between factory units and sewage works, with no overlooking vantage points. So this shot, from the leading dmu on the RCTS 'West Midlands' railtour of 22nd November, 1980 is particularly interesting. The view ahead shows the straight road continuing to Water Orton, whilst the track to the right leads to Castle Bromwich Junction. Notable is that both of these chords had been singled by this date, whilst the WWMJR westwards remained double track. *R. Monk*

the north and south, both originally on double track lines. Here both lines cross an area once occupied by the substantial works of the Birmngham Tame and Rea District Drainage Works, with its numerous sewage beds and water purification systems. A signal box was opened here with the line, on the northern side directly opposite the junction, but was replaced by the standard MR box on 18th January, 1903, and this was replaced by a standard LMS gable-ended box on 5th September, 1939, which survived until 10th August, 1969. The northern chord runs for 69 chains (just over ¾ mile), crossing the River Tame on the bridge that had caused Firbank so many problems in construction, to join the MR Birmingham-Derby main line at Water Orton West Junction. Meanwhile, the southern chord runs for 1 mile 26 chains (just over 1¼ miles) to join this line at Castle Bromwich Junction, close to Castle Bromwich station, although it does (and always did) run parallel to the main line for around half a mile before actually making the junction.

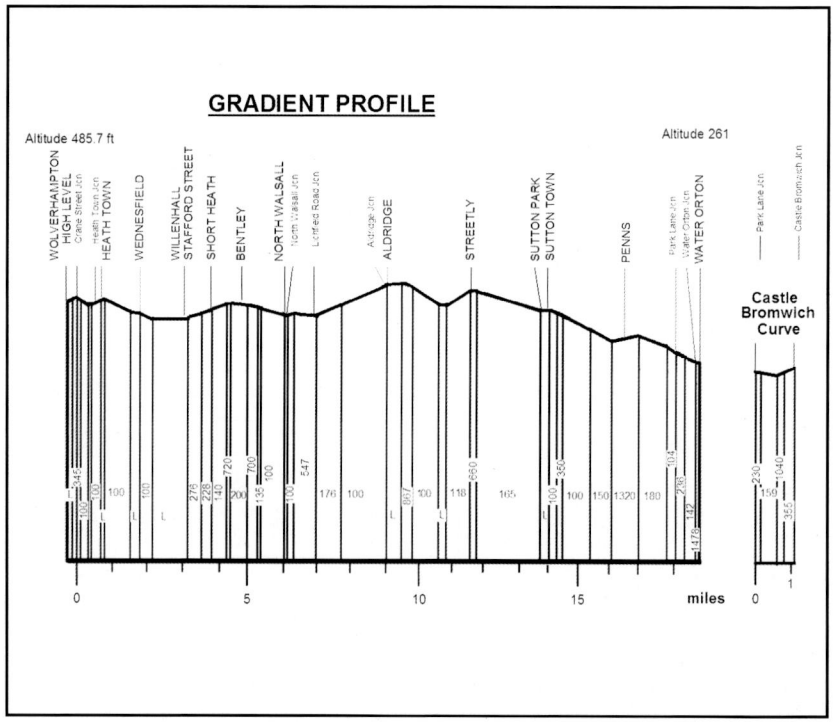

Gradient profile redrawn by the author from the Midland Railway 1902 plan.

Courtesy National Archive

Chapter Six

Working the line, 1879-1965

Passenger services

As mentioned in Chapter One, when the MR took over the WWR line in 1876 they immediately improved the level of services from 8 to 14 up trains and 9 to 15 down trains on weekdays, and three each way on Sundays. This pattern remained through to 1879 prior the opening of the WWMJR. However, with the opening of the new line, it was evident that some changes would be made, as many of the trains would run to or from Birmingham New Street, necessitating a reversal at Walsall. No trains were ever scheduled to run direct from Wolverhampton to Birmingham avoiding Walsall, as the possibility of attracting any through passengers was severely limited by the additional mileage that this route involved. For example, from Wolverhampton High Level to New Street via the LNWR Stour Valley route it was 12 miles 74 chains (say 13 miles), but via the WWR and WWMJR direct route, then the MR Derby main line from Water Orton, it was 24 miles 38 chains (say 24½ miles). By February 1883 the service pattern was:

	Weekdays		Sundays	
	Up	Down	Up	Down
Wolverhampton and				
Walsall	0	0	0	0
Birmingham	7	7	2	1
Derby	2	3	0	0
Walsall and				
Birmingham	5	5	1	2
Derby	1+1 SO	1	0	0

So it can be seen that workings solely between Wolverhampton and Walsall had been curtailed, and although the total number of trains on the WWR section remained about the same, they were extended along the WWMJR to Birmingham or Derby. By October 1890 the situation remained principally the same, with the addition of two or three trains each way between Wolverhampton and Walsall but no through trains to/from Derby:

	Weekdays		Sundays	
	Up	Down	Up	Down
Wolverhampton and				
Walsall	3	2	1	2
Birmingham	8	7	2	1
Derby	0	0	0	0
Walsall and				
Birmingham	2+1 SO	3	1	2
Derby	0	0	0	0
Sutton Park	1 SO	0	1	0

SO - Saturdays only.

However, the reintroduction of the Walsall-Wolverhampton service had resulted in a reduction in trains between Walsall and Birmingham. It will be noted that there are several unbalanced workings, also requiring empty stock workings to complete the round trips. The service to Sutton Park was operated only at weekends, to enable trippers to visit this popular beauty spot; it is presumed that passengers from outside the area would have to return on normal through trains to, for example, Birmingham. The Derby services had all been withdrawn - evidently the MR attempt to attract northbound passengers on to its system at Derby had failed. Indeed, by this time the LNWR were running services from Wolverhampton to Burton and Derby via the Portobello and Pleck curves, then along the SSR through Lichfield to join the MR route northwards at Wichnor Junction. By July 1906 the situation had changed substantially:

	Weekdays		Sundays	
	Up	Down	Up	Down
Wolverhampton and Walsall	1+1 SO	1+1 SO	0	0
Birmingham	10	10	5	5
Walsall and Birmingham	4	4	0	0
Sutton Park	1	0	0	0
Penns	1	1	0	0

Workings to Sutton Park remained a feature, at least during the summer months. It is believed that the working between Walsall (7.45 am) and Penns was a 'workmen's train', and a footnote in the working timetable stipulates that 'Engine is tender first to Penns, runs to Penns Goods to run round train'. Also of interest, is that the Sunday departure from Wolverhampton at 11.20 am was given as an 'express' service, completing the trip non-stop to Walsall in 15 minutes (normally 25 minutes), and onwards to Birmingham in an overall time of 44 minutes (normally 55-60 minutes).

Obviously, the competition from the LNWR between Walsall and Wolverhampton (as well as onwards to Birmingham) needed to be addressed. An agreement was reached between the MR and LNWR to eliminate wasteful trips between these two towns. Part of the problem was that any such workings solely using the lines of one of the companies would need a reversal in Walsall, if they were to proceed to or from Birmingham. However, if they were to cooperate, they could run through services without reversal using one part of, say, the MR route and then the next part on the LNWR route, or vice versa. So that is was occurred - or at least, in part. The agreement to pool competitive traffic was to last for 100 years, covered many goods and passenger services across the country and was dated July 1908. From the following 1st January the Lancashire & Yorkshire Railway was also included in this agreement. The LNWR was at this time operating its Walsall-Wolverhampton services solely on the route via Pleck and Portobello curves, so calling at Pleck, James Bridge (for Darlaston) and Willenhall Bridge stations.

The new arrangement applied to the route between Walsall and Wolverhampton only; trains to and from Birmingham continued to use the parent company's own route, as these served different local stations. The timetable for April 1910 can be summarized as follows:

	MR trains		LNWR trains	
	Up	Down	Up	Down
Weekdays				
Between Walsall and Wolverhampton				
Using MR route	5+1 SO	7+2 SO	3	2
Using LNWR route	4	1	0	1
Sundays				
Between Walsall and Wolverhampton				
Using MR route	4	4	0	0
Using LNWR route	0	0	0	0

The Sunday trains between Walsall and Wolverhampton did not call at North Walsall and Short Heath. There were 12 MR trains between Birmingham and Walsall on weekdays (plus two Saturdays only), of which eight continued on to Wolverhampton. In the reverse direction, there were also 13 (plus one Saturdays only) of which nine originated from Wolverhampton. There was also one each on weekdays from Walsall to Sutton Park and Sutton Town in each direction, not shown in the table above.

Just two years later, the working timetable for July to December 1912 records four fewer up MR trains using the WWR route, replaced by two more up LNWR trains on this line. Otherwise the pattern remained basically the same.

World War I obviously had a severe affect on rail services, but the working timetable for January to June 1916 showed remarkably little change to the overall level of services, although once more there had been a change in the balance between those companies using the WWR line:

	MR trains		LNWR trains	
	Up	Down	Up	Down
Weekdays				
Between Walsall and Wolverhampton				
Using MR route	5+1 SO	1+1 SO	3	5
Using LNWR route	5	8	1	0
Sundays				
Between Walsall and Wolverhampton				
Using MR route	5	5	0	0
Using LNWR route	0	0	0	0

However, by the following year there was a distinct shortage of both men and materials, as a result of which the line between Sutton Park and Aldridge, some 4¾ miles, was reduced to a single line from 7th January, 1917. The three mile section of the WWR from North Walsall to Willenhall was also singled, as from 4th February that year. The rails were to be used in France, to support the troops and equipment in the eventual advance across Europe. Passenger services on both of these lines were also severely limited. Double track was restored to these two sections on 20th March, 1921 and 8th May, 1921 respectively.

A member of Johnson's '1102' class of 0-6-0T arrives in Aldridge station, probably with a train from Brownhills. The line to Brownhills is in the background curving away behind the large goods shed. Meanwhile, passengers are disembarking and parcels are unloaded, from a down train from Birmingham New Street. The date is believed to be around 1910. *Author's Collection*

Streetly station facing toward Walsall in the years immediately prior to World War I. A Deeley 'Flatiron' 0-6-4T is calling with a train for Birmingham New Street. The loop line running round the far left platform face was still *in situ*, together with the platform mounted signal box.
Lens of Sutton/R.S. Carpenter

With the onset of peace, it was sometime before the railways could return to normality, and the Liberal Government of the time was considering nationalization of the railways. In any event, a compromise was reached resulting in the Grouping of the railways into four main groups. The LMSR was formed with effect from 1st January, 1923 and comprised, amongst others, the MR and LNWR. In the meantime, during this discussion period, service levels had dropped in May 1920 :

	MR trains		LNWR trains	
	Up	Down	Up	Down
Weekdays				
Between Walsall and Wolverhampton				
Using MR route	1	2	0	0
Using LNWR route	4	0	4	5
Sundays				
Between Walsall and Wolverhampton				
Using MR route	2	2	0	0
Using LNWR route	0	0	0	0

There were also four services each way between Birmingham and Walsall on weekdays and one on Sundays, and two each way between Walsall and Sutton Park every day. Matters worsened by the following year, with just three trains from Walsall to Wolverhampton and four in reverse, all using the WWR line.

However, by July 1922 the situation had almost reverted to its prewar levels:

	MR trains		LNWR trains	
	Up	Down	Up	Down
Weekdays				
Between Walsall and Wolverhampton				
Using MR route	5	4	3	1
Using LNWR route	0	3	0	1
Sundays				
Between Walsall and Wolverhampton				
Using MR route	0	3	0	1
Using LNWR route	0	3	0	1

There were 10 trains each way between Walsall and Birmingham, of which half originated or terminated at Wolverhampton. There were three Sunday services each way, which all ran between Wolverhampton and Birmingham. It is evident that prior to the Grouping, the LNWR and MR had constantly been trying to find a middle course to even out the disparities in sharing routes, hence the changes occurring almost on a yearly basis between the LNWR route and the WWR.

At this point it is interesting to reflect on the effects of local tram (and later bus) services that had on passenger traffic in the area. An examination of MR *Returns of Traffic and Expenses at Stations* reveals the following patterns:

Sutton Park station during World War I, with the platform full of troops. It is believed that these had been undergoing exercises at nearby Sutton Park, and were therefore about to return to their bases, prior to going into combat. *Author's Collection*

A charming view in the early 1920s, as Deeley 'Flatiron' 0-6-4T LMS No. 2014 rolls through Sutton Park with a local service. The coaching stock comprises a set of four close-coupled non-corridor carriages, and two clerestory roofed bogie carriages. Does one of the bicycles in the foreground belong to the photographer? *R.S. Carpenter*

Station	Passenger numbers			
	1877	1892	1907	1922
Heath Town	23,065	39,831	13,246	closed
Wednesfield	37,463	74,673	54,850	23,923
Willenhall	149,339	91,645	80,323	34,046
Short Heath	13,264	8,228	6,805	5,010
Bentley	4,752	206	closed	
North Walsall	15,271	18,589	13,166	2,071
Totals	243,154	233,172	168,390	65,050

Whilst the number of trains had not altered greatly between 1877 and 1907, the decline in passenger numbers was severe. The worst affected were those nearest to the large towns at each end of the WWR. Willenhall's decline was caused by the opening of the LNWR Portobello and Pleck lines in 1881, followed by the electrification of the tram services to Wolverhampton in 1904.

Conversely, the development of the residential areas around Sutton Coldfield and Streetly for commuters to Birmingham and Walsall improved the passenger levels from the beginning of the 20th century. As an example, at Streetly in 1901 just 32 season tickets were sold, whereas by 1922 this had risen to 317.

All passenger services on the WWR line were withdrawn as from 5th January, 1931, but the stations and goods yards remained open for goods traffic. The line remained equipped for passenger working, right up until its final closure, with absolute block working in place between Heath Town Junction and Lichfield Road Junction and Ryecroft Junction. A maximum speed limit of 45 mph was imposed on this part of the route, although the section from Lichfield Road Junction to Ryecroft permitted 60 mph running. The WWMJR route meanwhile continued to thrive, and by July 1938 reached 12 passenger trains each way on weekdays and two on Sundays. During that summer, there were four each way between Walsall and Sutton Park Mondays to Fridays, rising to eight on Saturdays and seven on Sundays.

Little is known of the services during World War II, as very few working timetables seem to have survived. Disruption caused by enemy bombing raids undoubtedly occurred, but is difficult to trace as newspapers were not permitted to record where such disruption took place. For instance, the newspapers could interview residents and even give their names, but were not allowed to state where they lived. However, it is known that the WWR route was reopened to passenger traffic in July and August 1942, as the result of bombing damage near Bilston Street, Willenhall, which had partially blocked the LNWR line. This was almost certainly caused by the severe raids that hit the area during the two nights of 29th and 30th July, 1942. The *Express and Star* at this time simply recorded the raids as being 'somewhere in the West Midlands' and did not even mention the disruption to rail services.

After nationalization there was little change, and the timetable for 30th June to 14th September, 1952 shows six trains from Walsall to Birmingham (plus one more on Saturdays) and six in the opposite direction. One train in each direction started or terminated at Wolverhampton, running via the LNWR route. An interesting working was that the 6.35 am from Walsall to New Street on

Webb former LNWR 2-4-2T No. 6755 standing in the down platform at Aldridge some time in the 1930s, with a Birmingham to Walsall train. The first two carriages are of the LMS period I non-corridor variety. *Author's Collection*

Stanier class '4' 2-6-4T LMS No. 2444 runs into Sutton Park station with a peak time stopping train from New Street to Walsall during the 1930s. These engines were more than competent performers on this type of work involving short distances between stations. *Author's Collection*

The off-peak service between Walsall and Birmingham New Street in LMS and BR days comprised a three-coach set of non-corridor stock, as seen in this view. Stanier class '4' 2-6-4T No. 42448 rolls into the orderly station at Penns on 20th June, 1949 heading for Birmingham.
HMRS/ESR

Stanier class '4' 2-6-4T No. 42482 runs into Sutton Park station with a local service from Walsall to Birmingham New Street on 20th June, 1949. The crossover permitted access for up goods trains to the goods yard located on the down side.
HMRS/ESR

Short Heath station on a very murky day, 13th February, 1950. A Fowler class '3' 2-6-2T No. 40045 is passing with a local passenger train for Wolverhampton. At this time no passenger services used the line, so the working must have been diverted from the Portobello route. To the right of the station building, a proud parent holds a small baby up to the fence to watch the train pass. *HMRS/ESR*

A shot of the return working seen above, with No. 40045 heading towards Walsall on this grim day. The coldness of the February fog can almost be felt. Evidently the main station building has received some attention, with new exterior rendering suggesting that it had found a new lease of life, possibly as a residence of some sort. *HMRS/ESR*

Stanier class '4' 2-6-4T No. 42482 halts at Streetly station on 6th June, 1953 with a Walsall to Birmingham New Street stopping train unusually made up entirely of corridor stock, painted in the delightful carmine and cream of that BR era. *F.W. Shuttleworth*

Stanier class '4' 2-6-4T No. 42601 runs into Aldridge station with a Walsall to Birmingham train in the early 1950s. This was evidently a peak service, as the normal first three non-corridor coaches have been strengthened by an additional four corridor coaches. Even at this comparatively early date, the goods yard seems to have become overgrown. *W.A. Camwell*

Streetly station on 6th June, 1953, with Fowler LMS Compound 4-4-0 No. 41194 forming the unlikely motive power for a two-coach Birmingham to Walsall stopping train.
F.W. Shuttleworth

Saturdays was listed as containing through carriages to Kingswear (arrive 1.50 pm). On Sundays the only service was from Walsall to Sutton Park and return, with a shuttle service operating eight trains in each direction.

From 17th November, 1958 all passenger services were officially taken over by dmus, operated from depots at Ryecroft and Monument Lane, but the timetable remained unchanged. However, these were not the first dmus to have been seen on the line, as sets built by the Gloucester Railway & Carriage Co. had traversed the WWMJR on their way to Longsight, Manchester during the latter part of 1957. The new order was well received by the public, although steam still made appearances during the next couple of years, as the dmus suffered from reliability problems.

Around this time (1957/58) consideration was given to using the site of Penns goods depot for a new Motorail service that BR intended to operate from the Midlands to Stirling. In the event, the site adjacent to Sutton Coldfield station on the LNWR route to Lichfield was chosen. Passenger usage on the line in 1960 was steady, if unspectacular, with Streetly attracting 80-90 on weekdays and 50 on Saturdays, Sutton Park with 30-40 on weekdays and 20 on Saturdays and Penns at 40-60 weekdays and 20-30 Saturdays.

By 1962 the service had dropped to five each way between Birmingham and Walsall on weekdays, with the Sunday shuttles from Walsall to Sutton Park continuing, by now at strictly hourly intervals and taking 16 minutes for each journey. There were also two weekday parcels workings from Walsall to New Street, and one to Central Goods, Birmingham. In the opposite direction, one ran from Leicester London Road to Walsall, one from New Street to Sutton Park, and one (at 9.23 pm Saturdays excepted) from Sutton Park to Bristol

An unidentified BR Standard class '5' 4-6-0 runs through the cutting approaching Sutton Park with a down express passenger service around 1959. *Author's Collection*

Hughes/Fowler 'Crab' 2-6-0 No. 42761 hauls an up empty stock working at the approach to the site of Sutton Town station in 1962. It has just passed beneath the bridge in the background, which carries High Street over the line. *R.S. Carpenter Collection*

Fowler '483' class 4-4-0s Nos. 486 and 500 double-heading the first part of the 'Pines Express' at Ryecroft Junction Walsall, on a busy August Saturday in 1936. They have just come off the spur from Lichfield Road Junction. *T. Talbot Collection*

Probably the northbound 'Pines Express', or one of its associated reliefs, is headed by an unidentified 'Jubilee' 4-6-0 racing through Sutton Park station, during 1960. *Author's Collection*

Temple Meads. This latter ran via Walsall, Wednesbury and the SSR to Dudley and Worcester.

In the last complete year of passenger workings, up to 14th June, 1964, services remained the same, with the timings only changing slightly. As from Monday 18th January, 1965 all passenger facilities on the WWMJR line were withdrawn and so the stations at Aldridge, Streetly, Sutton Park and Penns were closed from that date. Prior to this closure, some efforts had been made to attract further passenger traffic. Two halts were proposed around 1963 on the line. One was to have been at Coleshill Lane (actually at Ebrook Road), a little to the south of the former Sutton Town station, and got as far as being pegged out. Another was to have been at Kingsbury Road (A38) adjacent to the vast Castle Vale housing estate, and near to Minworth. It may be remembered that this was once the scene of a residents' petition to the MR to include a station there when building the WWMJR. Regrettably, neither proceeded.

Parcels workings remained an important part of traffic in 1968. There were two daily (Mondays excepted) workings into Walsall (from Peterborough and Leicester), one through working from Bristol to Crewe, and one each way from Sutton Park to/from Birmingham (Central Goods and Curzon Street).

The 'Pines Express'

In my book *The South Staffordshire Railway – Volume 1* (Oakwood Press, 2010) I gave a history of the operation of this famous named train (pages 146-7), as it was the only named train to regularly be routed via Walsall. As this also traversed the WWMJR on its circuit around Birmingham, a brief résumé is given here.

From 1927 to 1933, this train called at Walsall to change engines on Mondays, Fridays and Saturdays. The route from Walsall northbound or southbound was over the WWMJR to Water Orton where it joined the MR Birmingham-Derby line, then via the Camp Hill line southwards (thus avoiding New Street station) to/from Bath and Bournemouth. In this period, it was normal procedure for engines from the northbound 'Pines Express' (and its frequent reliefs) to travel light engine to Saltley for turning and servicing. However, at particularly busy times in the summer, the engines (especially if they were double-headed) were turned on the triangle from Ryecroft-North Walsall-Lichfield Road Junction-Ryecroft, then serviced at Ryecroft shed. The larger engines could not be turned on this shed's turntable as it was not enlarged from 50 ft until 1933. However, from 1933 until 1937 the train did not call at Walsall, instead travelling via the Stour Valley line to Birmingham New Street, where engine changing took place. From 1937 until the outbreak of World War II, the train reverted to its original path via Walsall and the WWMJR. After the cessation of hostilities, the service was reintroduced as from 6th May, 1946, and apart from a brief suspension from January to Easter in 1947 (due to adverse weather conditions), continued until the final service ran on 8th September, 1962. In busy summer weekends there were often relief services run, which sometimes also involved engine changing at Walsall.

Fowler '4F' class 0-6-0 No. 44177 pulls away from Sutton Park station on 30th May, 1959 with a down freight. It is about to pass the goods yard and shed on the left-hand side. The lengthy size of the Post Office sorting building is apparent in this view. *R.S. Carpenter Collection*

At North Walsall Junction, a Fowler '4F' class 0-6-0 and a Stanier '8F' 2-8-0 put maximum effort into bringing their train of loaded coal wagons on to the more level section of line, as they head for Birchills power station around 1960. *R. Selvey*

Freight services

We have already seen that the MR withdrew its goods services operated by running powers over the SSR from Wichnor Junction to Walsall, as soon as the WWMJR route was opened to goods on 19th May, 1879. On the same day, it began operating goods trains from Walsall over the SSR to Dudley using running powers granted in 1867. However, it could not immediately expand the level of its services to Wolverhampton as the goods depots there and at Walsall were not complete at that time. It had still to rely on the LNWR facilities at these two towns until its own were ready. In addition, the new engine shed at Walsall was similarly not complete, so the LNWR shed at Long Road could not (or probably would not) have handled any additional servicing, as the LNWR's new shed at Ryecroft was also not yet ready. Consequently, the frequency of goods services initially remained basically unaltered.

In 1875 the MR had exercised its running powers over the WWR, with two daily goods from Burton at 4.05 am that reached Wolverhampton at 8.45 am and returned at 9.25 am, the second left Walsall at 8.05 pm and returned from Wolverhampton at 9.45 pm. The working timetable for 1st October, 1876 (the first after acquisition of the WWR by the MR) shows just one goods working in each direction: 6.30 am from Wichnor to Wolverhampton (arrive 8.30 am), with stops in Walsall, Bentley, Short Heath and Willenhall. This returned at 9.15 am, arriving in Walsall at 10.00 am. The GWR goods also ran between Wolverhampton and Walsall (*see below*).

The MR goods services between Walsall and Wolverhampton never really reached any great levels, as during 1890 there were still only two on weekdays to Wolverhampton, with one returning and two on Sundays. By July 1906 this had dropped to one each way weekdays only, and had only risen by 1920 to three each way weekdays only, with an extra on Wednesdays only. There were also spasmodic workings from Walsall and Wolverhampton to Willenhall and/or Wednesfield at various times. However, other goods traffic did reach Wolverhampton via the direct line between Lichfield Road Junction and North Walsall. In 1890 there were a further three trains using this route each way on weekdays, rising to four in 1906 and staying at that number in 1920. By the end of the 1930s, the numbers had risen slightly to seven up and six down on weekdays, with one up on Sundays. However, in Summer 1958 this was four up and two down (plus one down on Sundays), but for September 1958 to June 1959 only one up and two down workings traversed the direct line. There were a further five each way between Wolverhampton and Walsall using the WWR. These included pick-up goods services on the Wolverhampton route, as well as coal trains and returning empties between Birchills power station and various Cannock Chase collieries.

It should also be noted that in the 1958/59 period a number of goods workings found their way from the Bescot direction, using the Portobello curve to Heath Town Junction, and thence into the MR goods depot at Wolverhampton. In addition, several workings called at both Wolverhampton LNWR Goods and the former MR depot. At this time there was a total of five such up workings daily, and six daily down, plus a further two Mondays excepted. Some of these were later reclassified as trip workings.

Bowen-Cooke '7F' 0-8-0 No. 49403 pauses during shunting operations at Wolverhampton's Wednesfield Road goods yard on a bitterly cold day, 16th February, 1963. Ice was still in evidence between the rails and sleepers, making walking rather hazardous on uneven surfaces. The LNWR line from Heath Town Junction to Wolverhampton High Level can be seen on the skyline in the background.
Author

Ivatt class '4' class 2-6-0 No. 43002 assists a Stanier '8F' class 2-8-0 with a coal train to Birchills power station, and have just passed beneath Mill Street bridge near to Ryecroft depot. The two locomotives are coupled back-to-back, so that on reaching Birchills, they can be separately detached to shunt the wagons into the power station sidings, then return with a load of empty wagons.
R. Selvey Collection

Representing the motive power and coal traffic that were typical of the line, an unrecorded Bowen-Cooke 0-8-0 powers up the bank from Ryecroft Junction to North Walsall Junction at Sandhills with a string of empty steel-bodied coal wagons. *R. Selvey*

A busy scene at Lichfield Road Junction, as a Stanier '8F' class 2-8-0 struggles up the 1 in 100 with a freight for the Water Orton direction. In the background, one of the area's ubiquitous Bowen-Cooke 0-8-0s waits on the WWMJR direct line from North Walsall Junction.
R. Selvey Collection

A very atmospheric view from inside North Walsall Junction signal box. A tender-first Stanier 'Black Five' 4-6-0 assists a Stanier '8F' class 2-8-0 up the grade from Ryecroft with a heavy coal train bound for Birchills power station, around 1963. *R. Selvey*

The platforms at Willenhall Stafford Street station were very overgrown by 1964, as Fowler '4F' class 0-6-0 No. 44218 pauses with a local freight from the Wolverhampton direction. The shunters are about to divide the train, so that it can be shunted into the goods yard on the left of the signal box. *R.S. Carpenter*

Slightly outside the scope of this book, but it is worth mentioning that in contrast, the MR goods services on the SSR line between Walsall and Dudley had positively boomed, with five each way on weekdays in October 1876, 11 southbound and eight northbound in October 1890, steadying at eight each way in July 1906. However, this all came to a halt with the introduction of the traffic sharing agreement of 1908, when the MR withdrew its goods services to Dudley as from 1st January, 1909.

There were additional goods workings between Walsall and Water Orton (traffic from the north) and Castle Bromwich Junction (traffic from the south), via the WWMJR after its opening, as follows :

	Weekdays		*Sundays*	
	To Walsall	From Walsall	To Walsall	From Walsall
October 1890	10+1 SO	8+2 SO	2	0
July 1906	12+1 MO	12+1 MO	4	0
July 1912	3+2 MX	3+1 MX	2	0
June 1916	4+2 MX	2+1 MX	1	0
May 1920	7	3	1	0
July 1939	6+3 MX	6+3 MX	1	0
July 1958	6+3 MX +1 SO	4+5 MX+3 SX +1 TThO	0	1

MO - Mondays only, MX - Mondays excepted, SO - Saturdays only, TThO - Tuesdays and Thursdays only

Not included in these figures are the pick-up goods workings that generally ran from Washwood Heath (via Castle Bromwich) or Water Orton to serve Penns, Sutton Park and terminated at Aldridge. These varied over the years, but were never more than two each way per day, and often just one. Sometimes, a service to Aldridge involved the locomotive in a spell on the Brownhills branch, and occasionally this involved returning light engine to Saltley shed - or even vice versa. There was no particular pattern for these pick-up goods, which as might be expected, were scheduled to satisfy to the demands of the local businesses. During the 1950s these were eventually treated as trip workings.

Traffic on the line from Lichfield Road Junction to North Walsall was increased during 1963/64 when the section between Ryecroft and North Walsall was relaid. So during this work, coal for Birchills was routed out of Walsall up to Lichfield Road, where an additional locomotive was added at the rear, which after reversal became the front of the train, the ensemble then traversing the direct line through to Birchills. Occasionally, such trains were propelled by one or two locomotives, obviating the need to add a further locomotive to the rear. The returning empties also, of course, would have traversed this route. Subsequently, the usefulness of the direct line was compromised by the severing of the WWR for the construction of the M6 motorway in September 1964. So the Lichfield Road Junction to North Walsall line was closed as from 1st January, 1965. However, this section of line was not taken out of use until 30th April 1967, closing officially the following day. Meanwhile, the section from Ryecroft Junction to Birchills power station remained in use until 12th May, 1980.

Stanier '8F' class 2-8-0 No. 48382 hauls a lengthy freight through Sutton Park on 12th December, 1964. It is probably heading for the extensive yards at Washwood Heath. *R.J. Buckley*

613.
Fowler '4F' 0-6-0 No. 44139 is engaged in shunting from the main WWR running line into the works of Ductile Steels Ltd at Wednesfield on 22nd May, 1965, just two months before this firm purchased a second-hand Ruston Hornsby type '48DS' 4-wheel diesel-mechanical shunter.

D. Bathurst

Freight traffic also dropped off dramatically in the 1960s with the increased move towards road haulage and the construction of motorways. The BR policy of ignoring partial wagon loads, then complete wagon loads, in favour of block trains of product did not help matters. The following table illustrates the number of freight movements over the WWMJR in this troubled period, and how it gradually improved. Light engine movements and trip workings are excluded, but the through workings to Birchills power station in 1962 are included, although these became trip workings after 1964.

	Mon	Tues	Wed	Thu	Fri	Sat	Sun
18th June, 1962-9th September, 1962							
Up	9	13	13	13	13	9	2
Down	7	10	10	10	9	11	-
4th October, 1965-Until further notice							
Up	4	7	6	8	6	4	-
Down	6	6	7	6	6	3	1
3rd October, 1966-5th March, 1967							
Up	6	8	8	8	7	4	1
Down	3	9	9	10	9	9	2
6th March, 1967-1st October, 1967							
Up	7	14	13	13	12	7	1
Down	6	13	13	14	14	10	2

	Mon	Tues	Wed	Thu	Fri	Sat	Sun
6th October, 1969-3rd May, 1970							
Up	9	15	15	15	15	12	-
Down	15	21	20	20	20	23	-
4th May, 1970-4th October, 1970							
Up	16	24	23	24	23	8	-
Down	15	28	27	28	27	26	-
3rd May, 1971-3rd October, 1971							
Up	8	10	13	12	11	12	-
Down	12	16	18	16	15	23	1
4th October, 1971-6th May, 1972							
Up	9	12	12	12	13	9	-
Down	18	20	21	20	20	12	-

One of the other reasons for the change in traffic patterns in this period was the modernization of the yard at Bescot, resulting in flows of goods to and from destinations not hitherto seen. Whereas previously, goods traffic had emanated from places on the former MR and LNWR systems, it had by the 1970s become much more long distance and 'inter-regional'. This was one benefit of the BR strategy introduced at the time, and which does seem to have had a continuing effect. Mind you, it had taken BR nearly 30 years to become much more of a national railway system.

It is not really practical to go into further detail as to the origins and destinations of goods traffic over the period from 1930 to the present day, due to the sheer number of such workings and the applicable origins and destinations. Any attempt would involve considerable duplication and become rather repetitive.

One further comment concerns signalling on the WWR line. From the late 1920s it would appear that it became regular practice at certain times of the day and night to switch out the boxes at North Walsall and Birchills Sidings, so that the section from Willenhall to Lichfield Road Junction was left as a through route. Similarly, the boxes at Willenhall and Wednesfield were only opened as required (especially in later years), with relief signalmen travelling in pick-up goods trains to operate the boxes whenever necessary.

Certain local speed limits have been noted elsewhere, but the overall speed limit for the WWR section by 1960 was given as 45 mph, and the Sectional Appendix at this time notes that the line was worked by absolute block control, so that the line was equipped for passenger working, even though no such services were booked.

Present day goods traffic over the WWMJR continues to show a solid growth, and there is every reason to expect the line to remain busy, with traffic turning north or south at the Water Orton end of the line, and from Bescot in a variety of directions. This line has become an important artery for freight traffic changing direction from the north-west/south-east corridor to the north-east/south-west corridor.

Trip workings

As might be expected with a number of local goods yards that were only sporadically served by regular goods trains, and a number of goods yards and private sidings to shunt, there were a number of local trip workings, most of which were not shown in the working timetables, but by way of trip notices. However, some were recorded as notes in various working timetables. For example, the 1909 MR working timetable notes that the 9.45 am Wolverhampton to Walsall goods was to make a trip to and from the Canal Basin at Wolverhampton as required, and before departure from Wolverhampton Goods. The 10.30 am Water Orton to Wolverhampton arrived at 12.20 pm, then shunted the Midland Basin [sic] and Mill Street (LNWR) goods depot as required. The engine for the 10.20 pm from Wolverhampton to Washwood Heath was to make a trip to and from the Canal Basin as required, before starting the train.

Tim Shuttleworth recalls that the shunt at Wolverhampton goods depot was a Bushbury shed turn, performed by LNWR 'Coal Tanks' prior to World War II, then by LNWR 0-6-0s. Eventually, when some former MR class '2F' 0-6-0s were allocated to Bushbury these were used. However, the former LNWR 0-8-0s were much more sure footed and came to dominate this turn, even after Bushbury shed closed and the duty was taken over by Bescot shed. In January 1964, No. 48895 from Bescot was a regular performer on this duty and six months later three members of this class were maintained for this task. However, Fowler 'Jinties' had often been used by Bushbury and Bescot sheds when no '7F' was available. In the closing years of steam, other classes were pressed into action, such as the BR Standard class '4' Moguls. Eventually, this duty fell to the class '08' 0-6-0 diesels until the regular shunting turn was discontinued, and any shunting work performed by locomotives on trip workings. Examples of local trip workings from 1959 and 1962 are given in *Appendix Two*.

Locomotives

Early passenger locomotives operated by the LNWR on the WWR services would have included Ramsbottom and Webb 2-4-0s of the 'Samson', ' Newton', 'Precedent', 'Jumbo', 'Whitworth' and 'Waterloo' classes, all of which are known to have appeared at Walsall on passenger trains, albeit mostly on the SSR route. But almost any of the earlier LNWR express locomotives may have operated here, once they had been cascaded from main line duties due to the introduction of more modern motive power. There was a somewhat surprising lack of tank locomotives for passenger duties in this period (1872-76), until the introduction of Webb's 4 ft 6 in. 2-4-0Ts, introduced in 1876. However, a relatively small number of 2-4-0Ts of the 'Crewe-type' were built by Ramsbottom and may well have also been suitable for the Wolverhampton to Walsall trains.

From the MR takeover of the line in 1876, and the opening of the WWMJR in 1879, it again seems likely that the MR employed 2-4-0s of the designs by Matthew Kirtley and later by Samuel Johnson. As for the LNWR, any of the MR express locomotives superseded by new designs were likely to be used in their dotage. The MR also had a lack of small passenger tank engines at this time, but this was soon remedied with the introduction of Johnson's 0-4-4Ts built in increasing numbers from 1878 until 1900. The MR shed at Pleck had a long association with both of these types. Later the Deeley 0-6-4Ts known as 'Flatirons' appeared on the trains to Birmingham New Street, some being allocated to Pleck and then Ryecroft sheds, as well as Saltley, which had been the parent shed for Pleck. Johnson and Deeley 4-4-0s of both classes '2' and '3' were at Pleck, and so probably saw use on the trains to Birmingham. Kirtley '170' class 2-4-0 No. 177 was shedded at Pleck prior to the Grouping and, prior to World War II, the MR presence in Walsall was represented at Ryecroft by Johnson MR '1262' class 0-4-4Ts Nos. 1249, 1250 and 1251 (LMS 3017, 3018 and 3019), Deeley 'Flatirons' MR and LMS Nos. 2036, 2037 and 2038, Johnson '1102' class half-cab 0-6-0T MR No. 1420 (LMS 1690) and Johnson '1873' class 0-6-0s MR Nos. 2056, 2133 (LMS 3333, 3410). Following the Grouping, the LMS used former LNWR Webb 5 ft 6 in. 2-4-2Ts on the Wolverhampton trains.

In the 1930s the Fowler, and later Stanier, 2-6-2Ts were allocated to Ryecroft for use on local services, including the WWMJR route. Later still, the larger 2-6-4Ts by Stanier and Fairburn were commonplace, but less so the Fowler version, although some allocated to Saltley occasionally appeared. Ivatt class '2' 2-6-2Ts were notable for working push-pull formations of up to four carriages on the

LNWR Webb 'Dreadnought' class 2-2-2-0 Compound No. 648 *Swiftsure* standing in Walsall station in 1903. In the background, MR Johnson '1262' class 0-4-4T No. 1277 stands at one of the platforms normally used by MR trains. This engine had a particularly long life, not being withdrawn until September 1950 at the ripe old age of 74 years. *R.S. Carpenter Collection*

This venerable Kirtley double-framed 2-4-0 bearing LMS No. 20008 was photographed at Ryecroft shed. It had been built at Derby in June 1867 originally being numbered 106. After rebuilding in 1881 and 1895, it was renumbered as MR No. 8 in December 1907, and received the LMS number 20008 in May, 1934. The photograph can be dated to between 1935 and 1937, as it arrived at Ryecroft in 1935, and was allocated to the District Engineer at Walsall in 1937, where it received the name *Engineer Walsall*. Other members of this class were allocated to the MR shed in Walsall, and later to Ryecroft, so were frequent visitors to the WWR. *R. Selvey Collection*

This Johnson '1282' class 2-4-0 was actually the class leader as MR No. 1282, but is seen here at Walsall station in August, 1936 bearing its LMS number 157. It was built by Dübs in 1876, rebuilt at Derby in 1887 and 1900, and finally withdrawn in December 1939 bearing its second LMS number, 20157. For most of its LMS life it was allocated to Walsall, as shown here by the '3C' shed plate. *T. Talbot Collection*

Bowen-Cooke 0-8-0 No. 49430 standing on the 'wrong line' near to Birchills Sidings with a permanent way train on 12th March, 1961. The workers are apparently unloading new wooden sleepers from the wagon immediately behind the locomotive. Further evidence of their work can be seen in the form of rails lying alongside the opposite running line. Sister locomotive No. 48964 was assisting in the work on this day. *RCTS/PMB*

An unidentified Bowen-Cooke '7F' class 0-8-0 runs back down the bank from North Walsall Junction towards Ryecroft, after having given banking assistance to a northbound freight working around 1960. *R. Selvey*

Ivatt class '2' 2-6-0 No. 46425 runs light engine at Ryecroft Junction, having just come off the Sutton Park route at Lichfield Road Junction on 11th April, 1961. The Ford Brook (notorious for flooding) can be seen running parallel to the line, behind the engine. Thus the former inhabitants of the derelict house on the right, had hopefully moved to a more peaceful and salubrious setting. *RCTS/PMB Collection*

shuttle services from Walsall to Sutton Park in the 1950s. In fact, on Easter Monday 1955 (11th April) No. 41279 was engaged on this duty, along with Stanier 0-4-4T No. 41902, which had enjoyed a brief stay at Ryecroft during that year, primarily for use on the Walsall-Dudley shuttles. The BR standard types made few appearances, if at all, as, for example, Saltley only ever had one of the class '4' 2-6-4Ts allocated to it, and that was for less than a year.

Sometimes unusual events were observed, especially towards the end of steam. One such was the arrival at Penns of 'Royal Scot' class 4-6-0 No. 46110 *Grenadier Guardsman* in early 1962 when shedded at Saltley, working the local trip No. T51. It performed some shunting before going on to Walsall Wood Colliery as part of the working.

The introduction of dmus saw the appearance of Park Royal and Derby Lightweight units on to the services from Walsall to Birmingham, and these held sway until the withdrawal of passenger services in 1965. Meanwhile, almost any type of locomotive could turn up on diverted main line services, and excursions, which were often routed out of Birmingham on to secondary lines as far as possible, so as to reduce the track occupation on the main line routes.

Goods engines in the early days can only be surmised. Trevithick 2-4-0s from the LNWR's former Northern Division and McConnell 0-6-0s from the former Southern Division are known to have operated in the area. The MR had concentrated on the 0-6-0 layout for its goods work, and those introduced by Kirtley and Johnson dominated the MR system. After the Grouping the LMS continued with many of these at Ryecroft shed, mostly of the Johnson design, then designated as '2F' or '3F' classes, but soon joined by Fowler standard '4F' 0-6-0s. But increasingly the former LNWR 0-8-0s by Bowen-Cooke became associated with the area, especially on coal trains worked from the Cannock Chase pits. Incoming freights from further afield also introduced Stanier '8F' 2-8-0s and often the numerous Stanier 'Black Fives', more particularly on fitted freights. Other mixed traffic types, such as the Hughes/Fowler 'Crabs', Ivatt 2-6-0s of class '2' and class '4' also frequented the line. Standard class '9F' 2-10-0s regularly worked across the WWMJR to and from Bescot yard, and even some of the Riddles 'WD' 2-8-0s put in an appearance occasionally. However, due to weaknesses on several bridges on the WWR section, this part of the line was restricted to the use of Fowler '3F' and '4F' 0-6-0s and the former LNWR '7Fs'. Interestingly, this section retained rails in 30 ft lengths until around 1942 when, using Italian prisoners of war, it was relaid with heavier rails in 60 ft lengths.

Shunting engines at Pleck and Ryecroft were comprised mainly of the Johnson 0-6-0Ts with the early half-cab design, and the later Fowler development which became known as 'Jinties'. These reigned supreme until the arrival of the BR Standard 0-6-0 diesel locomotives (later class '08') from the late 1950s onwards. These, along with diesel locomotives of classes '20', '24' and '25' were often used on local trip duties.

Into the diesel era, the first classes to make a debut were the BR-built class '24' Bo-Bos, soon followed by their successors of the class '25'. English Electric Bo-Bos of class '20' also became regular, along with Brush class '31' A1A-A1A and English Electric type '4' (class '40') locomotives, then class '37' Co-Cos, and soon afterwards the evergreen class '47' Co-Cos. The BR 'Peaks' (both class '45' and

Bowen-Cooke former LNWR 0-8-0 No. 49173 standing at Heath Town Junction on the line into Wednesfield Road goods yard, Wolverhampton on 17th March, 1963. Behind, the old terraced houses had been cleared away, and new council houses built post war. *Transport Treasury*

603.
BR Standard class '4' 2-6-0 No. 76039 about to depart from Wednesfield Road goods yard on 21st October, 1965 where there is evidently a crew change taking place. On the extreme right, part of the goods yard had been taken over by a local scrap merchant. *F.W. Shuttleworth*

'46') were also regular visitors, and the first known such visits were by Nos. D21 and D91 which had been at Saltley for crew training in March 1961, travelling from Castle Bromwich to Aldridge as part of this programme. But almost any type could, and eventually did turn up, such as WR 'Hymek' and 'Western' diesel hydraulics. Both the Romanian and British built class '56' locomotives were regulars; later on the relatively short-lived class '58' locomotives were commonplace, and their successors, the class '60' engines. Nowadays, it is the standard General Electric class '66' that is seen most often, with the newest class '70' variant also sometimes turning up.

Rolling stock

The early LNWR trains on the WWR were formed of their 4-wheeled stock, and those of the MR were of a similar design. The MR had abolished second class in its passenger vehicles from 1st January, 1875 and its carriage & wagon superintendent, Thomas G. Clayton, had reviewed the designs during the next year, eventually deciding (with Board approval) to go straight to bogie carriage design, missing out on the 'interim' stage of 6-wheeled vehicles altogether. Thus the MR was at the forefront of this design, which eventually saw its way into use on suburban trains. It is not known when such stock was in introduced to this area, but it must have been before the opening of the 20th century. Mostly the trains were composed of non-corridor carriages, and this policy continued during the LMS years, although corridor trains or mixtures of both types often occurred. This practice continued throughout the BR era up to the introduction of dmus in 1958.

GWR goods

As we have already seen, GWR running powers were granted over the WWR as from 1st September, 1867, but the GWR was not believed to have used these powers until 1875. The earliest workings that have been traced date from October 1876, after the acquisition by the MR of the line. There were two daily goods workings from Wolverhampton to Walsall, one in the morning (Mondays excepted) leaving at 6.10 am (Heath Town Junction) arriving in Walsall at 6.40 am, presumably at the LNWR goods depot at Long Road. The GWR eventually leased the southern half of this goods depot. This working returned at 7.40 am arriving in Wolverhampton half an hour later, which was to become the standard time for the trip. However, as the GWR was entitled to convey and/or collect traffic at Willenhall and Wednesfield such journey times may have been rather variable. The second working was in the evening, leaving Wolverhampton at 6.20 pm, and Walsall at 8.20 pm. Presumably, the locomotive was serviced as necessary at the LNWR shed at Long Road, adjacent to the goods depot.

By February 1883 timings of these workings were only altered by a few minutes, but the morning goods ran every day and an additional working was scheduled to be run 'as required'. The path for this was a 9.25 am departure from Wolverhampton and 10.40 am return from Walsall. In October 1890 the situation remained the same, but the 'as required' working now left Wolverhampton at 11.35 am, returning at 12.50 pm from Walsall. By July 1906 the morning goods had reverted to being 'Mondays excepted', but otherwise the schedules were unchanged. However, following World War I the 'as required' working was dropped, and in May 1920 the morning working returned to daily operation and the evening working was scheduled to run on Tuesday, Thursday and Friday only. An allowance of an extra 15 minutes for shunting at Wednesfield and Willenhall was introduced for this evening working.

After the Grouping, the pattern reverted to two daily weekday trains. The 1924 GWR working timetable shows that the first train left Oxley yard at 6.35 am, pausing in Wolverhampton from 6.43 until 7.06 am, then calling at Willenhall (Market Place) where shunting took place from 7.20 until 7.32 am. A further call was made at Short Heath from 7.35 for 10 minutes, and arrival in Walsall Goods was at 8.05 am. The return left at 9.40 am, calling at Willenhall from 10.35 until 10.50 am, at Wednesfield at 10.55 am for 15 minutes, with arrival in Wolverhampton at 11.25 am and Oxley rather surprisingly at 12.20 pm after having spent 50 minutes languishing in Cannock Road sidings. The afternoon working left Oxley at 4.30 pm, calling at Willenhall (4.50/5.00), and Short Heath (5.03/5.18) and Walsall 6.00 pm. This returned at 7.45 pm, with no shunting times allowed at the intermediate stations, arriving in Wolverhampton at 8.25 and Oxley at 8.35 pm.

These workings were suspended during World War II, and do not seem to have been resumed afterwards. Indeed, there would have been no need for them after nationalization.

Locomotives used on these turns were undoubtedly the Dean and Churchward 0-6-0STs, and possibly the pannier tank variants, including those by Collett in the later years. The LMSR enginemen at Walsall referred to them as 'Fattie Greenies', on account of their green liveries, and the saddle tank shape making them appear more rotund than the familiar MR and LNWR types. Their shrill GWR whistles also cause derision from their LMS colleagues at Ryecroft shed, when they latterly came for servicing.

Excursions

From almost the earliest days of rail transport, excursions had been put on for working people to visit, in the first instance, local events. As in the 1850s and 1860s most working people had only Sunday as leisure time, such excursions could only be limited. As time progressed, working weeks became shorter, and disposable income improved so such excursions became more frequent, and the destinations more adventurous. Eventually, of course, people were able to take a week's holiday away from home and special trains were organized to take people from this area to the South-West, to North and South Wales and to the Lake District, to give but a few examples. The MR was keen to develop its new route from Wolverhampton (via the WWR and WWMJR) for this purpose. The following are advertisements from the *Wolverhampton Chronicle* of 25th June, 1879 (originals not suitable for reproduction):

MIDLAND RAILWAY
NEW ROUTE TO LONDON
HORTICULTURAL SOCIETY'S SHOW and
GOOD TEMPLARS' and TEMPERANCE FETES

COOK'S CHEAP EXCURSIONS to LONDON, as under: -
THURSDAY, July 3rd, from WOLVERHAMPTON (High Level) at 10.10 a.m., Willenhall (Market-place) 10.20, North Walsall 10.34, Walsall 10.50, and Sutton Coldfield (Town Station) 11.14 a.m., for three, five, six, or seven days.

SATURDAY, MONDAY, and THURSDAY, July 5, 7 and 8, from WOLVERHAMPTON at 5.15 a.m., Willenhall 5.24, North Walsall 5.32, Walsall 5.40, and Sutton 5.58 a.m. Cheap Day Trips each day. Tickets also issued on Saturday to return Monday, Tuesday, or Wednesday ; on Monday to return Tuesday or Wednesday ; and on Tuesday to return Wednesday.

TUESDAY, July 8, DAY TRIP to the CRYSTAL PALACE for Good Templars' and Temperance Fetes.

SUTTON PARK RACES

CHEAP EXCURSIONS, by the new direct route, to STREETLY (near the racecourse) and SUTTON (Park Station), on TUESDAY and WEDNESDAY, July 1 and 2. Tickets and bills at COOK'S New Tourist and Excursion Office, Post Office Buildings, the Bridge, Walsall, and at the Stations

The following advertisements are from the *Walsall Chronicle* of 1st July, 1882:

MIDLAND RAILWAY
COOK'S CHEAP EXCURSIONS

Every MONDAY from Walsall, 8 am, DAY TRIPS to MATLOCK and ROWSLEY

MONDAY NEXT, July 17th. From Walsall 8.35am, Aldridge 8-45 and Sutton (Town) 8.55am, DAY TRIP to WORCESTER and MALVERN.

SATURDAY, July 22nd and MONDAYS, July 24th and 31st from Walsall 8 am, Aldridge 8.10am, and Sutton (Town) 8.20am. DAYTRIPS TO MATLOCK, ROWSLEY and BUXTON.

Monday, July 24th. From Walsall 6.30am, Aldridge 6.35 and Sutton (Town) 6.48am to LONDON and the CRYSTAL PALACE for 1 or 5 days, and to PARIS, &c, for 16 days.

DAILY (Sundays excepted) CHEAP EXCURSION BOOKINGS to STREETLY and SUTTON PARK.

Tickets and Bills at Cook's Tourist and Excursion Office, The Bridge, Walsall, and Midland Booking Offices.

LMS Fowler class '4F' 0-6-0 No. 4492 standing in the platform at Sutton Park having just worked in with an excursion for the park around 1948. The locomotive still bears its LMS number on the cabside and 'LMS' on the tender side. *Author's Collection*

The SLS special of 26th May, 1951 stands in Aldridge station after visiting the Brownhills branch, with Ivatt class '2' 2-6-2T No. 41226 sandwiched between the two auto-train sets. *HMRS/ESR*

MIDLAND RAILWAY
COOK'S CHEAP EXCURSIONS

SATURDAY, July 22nd, from Walsall, 6.35am, to BRISTOL, WESTON-SUPER-MARE, EXETER, TORQUAY, PLYMOUTH, PENZANCE, ILFRACOMBE, BATH, SALISBURY, BOURNEMOUTH, WEYMOUTH, SOUTHAMPTON, JERSEY, &c, for usual long period.

MONDAY, July 24th. Cheap SPECIAL EXPRESS from Walsall to LIVERPOOL by the New and Picturesque Route via Matlock, for 1,2,3, or 6 days.

Tickets and Bills at Cook's Tourist and Excursion Office, The Bridge, Walsall, and Midland Booking Offices.

Excursions continued right through into BR days, with those for holiday destinations really only disappearing in the 1960s with the spread of car ownership, and later the introduction of cheap foreign holidays.

Special workings

On 26th May, 1951 the Stephenson Locomotive Society (SLS) organized a tour of goods and minor lines in the West Midlands. This was powered by Ivatt 2-6-2T No. 41226 formed in the centre of two two-coach auto-train sets, and ran along the WWR from Wolverhampton to Aldridge, where it visited the Brownhills branch as far as Brownhills station, then continued back into Birmingham via Water Orton.

In connection with the centenary of the opening of the Oxford, Worcester & Wolverhampton Railway from Priestfield to Wolverhampton, a special train was run on 13th November, 1954 by the SLS, using Collett 0-4-2T No. 1438 (of Stourbridge Junction shed) and two 70 ft auto-trailers. It started from Birmingham Snow Hill, and after visiting Wolverhampton Low Level station took the chord line to Heath Town, then went along the WWR to North Walsall and into Walsall station, before continuing the remainder of its itinerary and returning to Snow Hill.

Services on the Lichfield-Aston ex-LNWR line were interrupted for several days following the serious accident on that line at Sutton Coldfield station on 23rd January, 1955. To facilitate passengers wishing to travel to and from Sutton Coldfield town centre, the closed Sutton Town station on the WWMJR line was reopened for three days, along with enhanced services.

From 1st-12th August, 1957 a World Scout Jamboree was held at Sutton Park. Around 170 special trains were used to bring scouts and visitors to the Jamboree, and to take those in camp on day excursions and industrial visits, which incidentally included both Crewe and Derby BR Works as well as the Cadbury factory at Bournville, Coventry car works and the cathedral. Trains had actually started arriving on 29th July and eventually peaked when they were arriving every 12 minutes. Overall 81,000 passengers were carried, with a further 1,390 coming by air. Those special trains used reporting numbers in the

Whilst the SLS special seen in the previous photo stands in Aldridge station, participants mingle on the station platform, as Stanier 'Black Five' 4-6-0 No. 45395 passes with the 4.40 pm Water Orton to Bushbury freight.
T.J. Edgington

The date is August 1957 and as part of the rather frantic workings for the Scout Jamboree, 'Jubilee' class 4-6-0 No. 45600 *Bermuda* runs into Walsall near to Pleck Junction with a working from north-west Lancashire to the Jamboree at Sutton Park.
R.S. Carpenter

series commencing M400 and W800, although some from other areas did carry numbers from their districts. This additional traffic was handled at Sutton Park and Streetly stations on the WWMJR, although some were routed to Sutton Coldfield and Four Oaks on the LNWR Aston-Lichfield line. As mentioned earlier, temporary block posts were set up at Streetly and Penns stations in connection with these workings. The block post at Penns was situated in an asbestos lamp cabin with two levers and block instruments, and was staffed by two relief signalmen working two 12 hour shifts. At Streetly, a special platform was constructed of sleepers about a mile towards Sutton Park for unloading baggage and equipment for the site. On Tuesday, 6th August alone 23 special trains were put on for 'Wolf Cub Day'.

The *Railway Observer* of September 1957 recorded many of the workings:

> The Scouts began to arrive on 29th July and trains from all parts of Great Britain were arriving all day. One working (W806) from Euston to Sutton Coldfield, unloaded and worked immediately via Wichnor Junction with the empty stock to Sheffield (Heeley). During the next two days the majority of traffic was from the Channel Ports and Parkeston Quay. On 30th July, four trains (M972-975) came from Dover to Sutton Park via Brent, Wigston and Water Orton and two from Newhaven reached Sutton Park via Willesden, Nuneaton and Water Orton, one of these trains (W819) was reported as an ambulance train and brought disabled Scouts from France.
>
> On 30th and 31st July some of the trains from Dover, Folkestone and Newhaven made a round trip. They ran to Sutton Coldfield via Willesden, Coventry, Stechford and Aston, unloaded and left immediately as empty stock for their S.R. carriage depots, travelling forward to Wichnor Junction, Coalville, Wigston, Hendon and Clapham Junction. The day the Jamboree opened, 1st August, a train conveying VIPs and hauled by Britannia 70045 *Lord Rowallan* (rep. No. M770) left St. Pancras at 10.35 am, travelled via Wigston and reached Sutton Park at 1.37 pm. The empty stock went on to Walsall and the locomotive to Bescot. This train returned from Streetly at 5.55 pm and arrived back at St Pancras at 9.27 pm. The next day, Rebuilt Royal Scot 46168 *Girl Guide* carrying a special smoke box headboard brought Guides in camp at Windsor on a visit to Sutton Coldfield. Most days special excursions were arranged for Scouts at the camp and to provide motive power BR class '2' 78055 and 2-6-4T 42118 were on loan to Bescot and Stanier class '5s' 45067, 45113, 45307/28 and 'Jubilee' 45666 *Cornwallis* were on loan to Walsall. Local train services were increased and six diesel car sets from Llandudno Junction (M79173/4/5/8/9/80 and trailers M79674/5/8/9/80/1) were on loan for working the Birmingham (New Street)-Lichfield line. (Petrol rationing, the bus strike and the Jamboree must have made this one of the most profitable services on British Railways.) The ordinary train service on the Birmingham (New Street)-Castle Bromwich-Walsall line was suspended and four coach push and pull sets used to work an increased service with several trains extended to Wolverhampton (High Level) and others to Dudley. Ivatt 2-6-2Ts 41212/20 and 41320/4 were on loan to Walsall to work this push and pull service. Other engines on loan for the two weeks were: 42935/53/76, 43022, 44911 to Bescot (3A), 42449, 42566, 45625 *Sarawak* to Bushbury (3B), 42885, 45073, 45130, 45249, 45424 to Aston (3D), and 41119/67 to Monument Lane (3E), bringing the total of 'borrowed' engines up to twenty-six. When the Jamboree closed the traffic arrangements for bringing the Scouts to the Jamboree were, generally speaking, put into reverse and by the next week-end the engines which had been on loan had returned to their own depots.

The BR Standard Pacific No. 70045 *Lord Rowallan* mentioned above, had been named in honour of the Chief Scout at a special ceremony at Euston station on 16th July. Many of the other workings will be of interest:

Thompson 'B1' class 4-6-0 No. 61205 brought in a special from Cambridge.
Both appropriate 'Royal Scot' 4-6-0s Nos. 46168 *The Girl Guide* and 46169 *The Boy Scout* were used on a number of workings.
No. 70045 worked in on a VIP train from St Pancras on 1st August.
'Black Five' No. 45333 (of the former Cheshire Lines Committee Brunswick shed, Liverpool) worked in from Baguley, Cheshire on 4th August.
'Black Five' No. 45061 worked in from Southport on 6th August.
'Jubilee' No. 45600 *Bermuda* worked from Millom in Cumbria to Streetly on 7th August.
'Royal Scot' No. 46135 *The East Lancashire Regiment* worked from Sutton Park to Newcastle.
Dispersal workings were made over 13th and 14th August.

Meanwhile, local services outside peak times were suspended and replaced by an interval auto-train worked by Ivatt 2-6-2Ts Nos. 41212, 41220, 41224, 41320 with BR Standard Mogul No. 78055 on longer trains.

On Saturday, 2nd June, 1962 a former LNWR Bowen-Cooke 0-8-0 (No. 48930 of Bescot shed) powered another SLS special from Birmingham New Street at 2.00 pm that visited many freight only and minor lines in the West Midlands. Included in the itinerary was a run from Wolverhampton Low Level up the connection to the WWR at Heath Town, then along this line to North Walsall, traversing the direct connection to Lichfield Road Junction, and onwards to Water Orton, eventually returning to New Street at 9.45 pm. The fare for the complete trip was 20s. 6d.

A year later, on Saturday 22nd June, 1963, another SLS special left New Street at 1.30 pm behind another Bescot '7F' 0-8-0, this time No. 49361, but on this occasion after running from Wolverhampton Low Level to North Walsall, it turned right into Walsall and then traversed lines in the Black Country and Cannock Chase before arriving back at New Street at 9.00 pm. The same fare applied.

Three months earlier, the Locomotive Club of Great Britain had sponsored a trip with a three-car dmu on Saturday 23rd March, 1963 from Birmingham Snow Hill at 11.30 am, which among the many lines visited ran along the WWMJR from Water Orton to Lichfield Road Junction and Walsall. It arrived back at Snow Hill at 5.20 pm. The fare was 25s.

Chapter Seven

Closure and retrenchment

In 1963 work on the M6 motorway threatened the future of the WWR line near Bentley. BR saw little future for the line, as in 1962 there were just five daily up workings Monday to Friday (plus one light engine movement) and three on Saturdays, with three down workings on all days. There was no Sunday traffic. All of these workings were fairly local and could be found alternative routes, if necessary. BR took the decision to agree to the severing of the line by the M6 works.

Therefore, the line from Ryecroft Junction to North Walsall and onwards to Heath Town was closed to through traffic as from 10th August, 1964. The line was actually severed near to milepost 49, north of Birchills power station on 28th September of that year, and on 7th December the section from Short Heath to Willenhall was taken out of use. The next section westwards, from Willenhall to Wednesfield was worked as a siding from 15th August, 1965, and Wednesfield goods depot officially closed on 4th October that year. However, official closure for the entire section between Birchills Sidings and Wednesfield was not made until 1st November, 1965 at which date Willenhall goods depot was officially closed. This line, eastwards from Wednesfield was removed prior to December 1971. The remaining western section of the WWR, from Wednesfield to Heath Town Junction was worked under the 'one engine in steam' regulations from 15th August, 1965.

Meanwhile, the WWMJR direct route from Lichfield Road Junction to North Walsall was starved of traffic, except for any workings to Birchills power station. However, there were very few such workings, as the majority of power station coal came from Cannock Chase via the SSR into Walsall, then entailing a reversal there. So traffic ceased on the Lichfield Road Junction to North Walsall line as from 7th June, 1965, although it was not taken out of use until 30th April, 1967, with official closure being the next day. Removal of the track did not occur until 1974.

As we have seen passenger traffic over the WWMJR between Walsall and Water Orton was withdrawn as from 18th January, 1965. Sutton Park goods depot had already closed, as from 7th December, 1964, but was taken over by the Post Office parcels depot which remained open. Aldridge goods depot closed on the same day. Penns goods depot closed as from 1st February, 1965. With only freight traffic, and the occasional diverted through passenger trains on the WWMJR, this was eventually downgraded to a goods line from 7th January, 1968. However, diverted passenger workings were still permitted, and certain summer workings on Friday evenings and Saturdays regularly used the line during the next 15 years or so. From the same date, the northern chord of the triangle at Park Lane Junction, connecting to the MR Birmingham-Derby line at Water Orton was singled, and the southern chord was altered to be worked by the absolute block system. The southern chord to Castle Bromwich was eventually singled as from 3rd August, 1969.

Two class '47' Co-Co diesel-electrics at the sidings adjacent to Birchills power station in the late 1960s. The nearest locomotive is No. 1629, which is working part of 9T54, a Bescot trip diagram. It has just propelled its loaded coal train from near Ryecroft Junction. But the identity of the other locomotive is not known, although its reporting number (9T52) discloses another Bescot trip diagram. *R. Selvey Collection*

A pair of English Electric class '20' Bo-Bos near to North Walsall Junction with coal from Coalville on working 8G20 for Birchills power station, around 1966. *R. Selvey Collection*

On the eastern section of the WWR, coal traffic had continued to serve Birchills power station. However, by 1970 most of the Cannock Chase pits had closed and what output remained no longer reached the power station. In 1971/72 there was a daily train (8G20) running Monday to Friday from Coalville at 9.25 am, requiring reversal in Walsall and arriving at Birchills at 11.24 am. The empties were worked back by duty 8P51 at 12.43 pm. The last working ran on 5th December, 1978, although it was not until 12th May, 1980 that the section from Ryecroft Junction was officially closed.

Returning to the western end of the WWR, a private siding in Wednesfield goods yard had been leased to Vialit & Company, but was removed by 17th July, 1966, and the remaining sidings in the goods yard by 1st May, 1967. The line from Heath Town to Wednesfield was mothballed at this time, but was reopened in July 1970 to Wednesfield a few hundred yards east of the station site, for steel traffic to the stockyard of a new £10 million tube mill of The Weldless Steel Tube Co. Ltd at Neachells Lane. Considerable earthworks were necessary, as the original line was on an 8 ft embankment at this point, but this was regraded and a new line laid on a falling gradient into the stockyard. Initially, three trains of 24 wagons per week ran from Round Oak Steelworks at Brierley Hill, carrying round steel bars of between 4½ in. and 6¼ in. diameter in lengths of between 20 and 30 feet. In 1969 these trains arrived at 8.00 pm on Monday, Wednesday and Friday, with the empties returning two days later at 4.16 pm. They were supplemented with trains from Scunthorpe daily at 6.12 am (MX) and 8.20 am (MO) with the empties returning at 8.10 or 8.35 am. By 1970 there were two Round Oak workings arriving on the same alternate days at 3.52 and 7.50 pm and the Scunthorpe train continuing at the same daily time. These workings continued for several more years at similar times, but eventually with the closure of Round Oak steelworks on 23rd December, 1982 this traffic ceased, and the line was severed at some 550 yards east of Heath Town Junction in November 1983. Thereafter all steel traffic was catered for at Wednesfield Road goods depot in Wolverhampton (*see Chapter Three*). The remaining track between Heath Town Junction and Wednesfield was removed during the Spring and early Summer of 1985.

Apart from this depot, the chord into Wolverhampton Low Level had remained in occasional use, even after the closure of the GWR route to Birmingham Snow Hill to passenger use from 4th March, 1972. The Low Level station had been converted into use as a Parcels Concentration Depot, opening on 6th April, 1970, even while the shuttle service to Snow Hill continued, but when that too ceased the depot was able to use the entire space. However, this parcels depot closed as from 1st June, 1981, with the last rail movement taking place on 12th June. The chord was taken out of use in October 1984, but was used as a siding for permanent way vehicles and a new maintenance depot constructed alongside. Since that time, the area encompassing the former yards of Wednesfield Road goods depot and the chord to Low Level station has been redeveloped as part of a huge Royal Mail sorting depot.

This chapter can end on a slightly more upbeat note, as the WWMJR line was upgraded to passenger status as from 2nd December, 1984. However, efforts by local transport groups have so far been unsuccessful in persuading either

A direct view eastwards along the WWR at Wednesfield on 10th June 1968. The station is crumbling, and the wooden goods shed alongside in a relatively dangerous condition. The original, low level of the platform height may also be observed. *D. Bathurst*

A view on 10th June, 1968 of Wednesfield station, with the remains of the wooden goods shed to the left. The red brick building behind is the gatehouse and offices of Jenks & Cattell on Neachells Lane. *D. Bathurst*

The MR hipped-roof goods shed at Wednesfield was being demolished on 17th May, 1970, when this photograph was taken. Its partly dismantled state gives an opportunity to examine the wooden construction. *M.A. King*

The inside of the partly dismantled goods shed at Wednesfield, displaying further details of its construction and the disposition of the internal loading platform. *M.A. King*

Minus its signal arm, this overhung bracket signal post is still of interest. The site is on the down line at Wednesfield, and the date is 17th May, 1970. *M.A. King*

English Electric type '4' (class '40') Co-Co diesel-electric No. 40005 propels a loaded coal train for Birchills power station between Ryecroft and North Walsall Junctions on 16th May, 1974. At this time, it became a regular, if unorthodox, practice for such trains arriving locomotive first in Walsall from the north, to be so propelled to the power station, to avoid running round the train. This also obviated the need for brake vans at each end of the formation.   *R. Selvey*

BR Standard 350 hp 0-6-0DE No. 08809 is seen here on 30th June, 1974 with a permanent way train removing the line between Lichfield Road Junction and Walsall North Junction. The Proffitt Street overbridge is in the background, and the arms of the track panel wagons can be seen to be slewed outwards, ready to remove track panels on the northbound line.   *R. Selvey*

A gaggle of class '20s' at Ryecroft Junction on 22nd December, 1975, just where the WWR met the SSR, with the site of the erstwhile locomotive shed just out of view to the left. Nos. 20072 and 20175, in the foreground, are in the process of propelling their loaded coal train towards Birchills, whereas Nos. 20075 and 20178 (behind) are returning from the power station sidings with an empty train. *R. Selvey*

BR Sulzer class '47' Co-Co diesel-electric No. 47227 heads a permanent way train on the section between Ryecroft Junction and North Walsall Junction in the 1970s. Certainly the track appears in urgent need of attention, especially as it was regularly used by trains to Birchills power station at that time. *R. Selvey*

An interesting view of the Sutton Park goods shed, yard and its approach lines on 22nd November, 1980. At this date, the goods shed and yard were still busy with traffic for the parcels service of the Post Office. This photograph was taken from the Metropolitan-Cammell dmu (50309+59121+50336) forming the RCTS 'West Midlands Reunion' railtour that travelled along the WWMJR from Walsall to Castle Bromwich as part of its complex itinerary. *R. Monk*

A smart new depot for permanent way vehicles was erected in Wolverhampton around 1983 about mid-way along the spur from Heath Town to the former GWR line, after parcels traffic had ceased at the former Low Level station. One such vehicle is stabled outside this depot, together with an attendant trolley. *S. Dewey*

Brush class '47' No. 47350 has become derailed on the spur from Heath Town Junction to the GWR Low Level at Wolverhampton on this day in March/April 1985. The breakdown train from Bescot has been called to assist, headed by a class '20', just visible at the far end. Judging by the number of 'Presflo' wagons stabled in the Wednesfield Road goods yard and the adjacent sidings, there was a considerable traffic in powder cement at this time. *S. Dewey*

During removal of a bridge at Deans Road near to Heath Town, Wolverhampton in May 1985, this contractor's mobile crane managed to over-reach itself whilst positioned on the WWR trackbed, with the consequences visible here. The hire firm, Ellis Crane Hire, would have not been very amused, and the job of righting the errant vehicle must have been rather awkward.
S. Dewey

Railtrack, Network Rail or any local government partnerships to reinstate passenger services, which would obviously necessitate expenditure on station facilities. It must be noted that since closure, most of the land near to the original stations has been built upon, and also this would make any such infrastructure (not forgetting the inevitable car parks) a difficult proposition.

However, a further outline proposal was put forward in 2011, for a 'train-tram' service to operate from Aldridge through to Stourbridge Junction. The intention was to give Aldridge a rail connection to Walsall (and thus also to Birmingham), with the unit then proceeding from Bescot on the trackbed of the SSR through Wednesbury to Dudley, Brierley Hill and Stourbridge. This latter stage would be Line 3 of the Midland Metro, and require units capable of tram style operation on this route.

Much freight activity continues to use the WWMJR route, and the future of the line as an important artery for this traffic is assured. In addition, this route has been used by a number of steam specials, mostly originating from the Birmingham Railway Museum site at Tyseley, and heading for a variety of destinations to the west (such as Ironbridge and the Severn Valley Railway) and the north-west (such as Chester and North Wales). The return workings have also traversed this route, as well as several light engine movements, where steam locomotives have run to Bescot to take up their workings. Other special workings involving the use of a variety of diesel locomotives, both in current use and restored, have also occurred.

View westwards from Reedswood Way, Walsall towards Willenhall, with all track lifted, 26th December, 1996. *R. Selvey Collection*

Chapter Eight

The Brownhills branch

The Brownhills branch ran from Aldridge through Walsall Wood to Brownhills, continuing alongside Chasewater to make a connection with the Cannock Chase and Wolverhampton Railway (CCWR) near to Conduit Colliery. This was built in two stages, and we will examine each. As this line was being planned and constructed at the same time as the WWMJR, administration of this project was also undertaken by the MR Walsall Branch Committee, although this line was referred to as the Walsall Extension Railway in some correspondence. When complete the entire branch was usually known as the Brownhills branch or Cannock Chase branch. A further short-lived branch connected to the LNWR Norton branch and to Coppice No. 6 and No. 8 pits at Wilkin, near Brownhills.

Walsall Wood branch

The MR Walsall Branch Committee met at Derby on 31st August, 1875 to consider the construction of a 'colliery branch from Aldridge Station' and decided to refer the matter to the MR Board. This matter was in turn referred to the Way & Works Committee, which on 14th September, 1875 suggested that connections could be made to Leighswood, Aldridge and Walsall Wood collieries. John Addison was selected as Engineer for the line, but on 4th July 1876 was instructed by the Walsall Branch Committee 'not to proceed making any arrangements whatever in respect of this line until after Royal Assent has been given to the Bill and the matter has been considered by this committee'. The Bill was before Parliament at the time, and approval for construction was eventually included in section 4 of the MR (New Works) Act, of 13th July, 1876 (Vict. 39 & 40, cap. 145). The line was specified as Railway No. 2 in this section as running 'from a junction at Aldridge with the railway from Water Orton to Walsall authorized by the WWMJR Act of 1872, in a field abutting on the road from Pelsall to Perry Barr near Red House to Paul's Coppice at Walsall'. This latter reference to Paul's Coppice (belonging to the Earl of Bradford) being at Walsall is misleading as it refers to the borough rather than the location, which is in Walsall Wood. The length was given as 2 miles 3 furlongs (just under 2½ miles) and five years were allowed for its completion.

On 5th December, 1876 John Addison was instructed by the committee to prepare plans, specifications and bills of quantities so that tenders from contractors could be obtained. However, on the following 6th March the committee was informed that the MR Board had decided 'not to proceed with the branch at the present time', this being communicated in their Board Minute No. 1342 dated 7th February, 1877. So everything was put on hold. However, Addison was evidently well aware of local circumstances, and reported on 3rd April, 1877 that the land to be used for the Walsall Wood branch was at present used as brickworks, and that to avoid any future leasehold problems, it could and should be purchased now. But, bearing in mind the Board instruction, the committee did not agree.

Evidently, having seen the Act go through Parliament and with nothing happening, the local businesses were becoming a little concerned, for on 2nd October 1877, a letter from the Aldridge Colliery Co. was read to the committee, requesting immediate construction of the branch. This seems to have stirred the committee into action, and on 6th November they instructed Addison to prepare the plans, and their land agent W. Fowler to purchase the required land. Fowler was to be paid 250 guineas (£262 10s.) for land purchase inclusive of expenses, plus 5 guineas (£5 5s.) per day for arbitration arising. On 4th December, Addison submitted his plans to the committee, which contained a revision to the original plans to avoid the leased lands of the Aldridge Colliery Co. that he had suggested eight months earlier could have been purchased. This deviation required Parliamentary approval, which was eventually obtained in section 4 of the MR (Additional Powers) Act, dated 17th June, 1878 (Vict. 41 & 42, cap. 96). The deviation was included as Railway No. 4 in this section and described as being 4 furlongs 8 chains 13 yards (½ mile) from a junction at Aldridge with the authorized line to field No. 29 on the original plans. Five years were given to make this deviation.

On 5th November, 1878 the committee were asked to approve the construction of sidings for the use of local tradesmen involved in the construction, presumably at Aldridge. However, the committee decided against this proposal, as the usual practice was that the main contractor furnished any such temporary sidings as part of his contract.

Finally, on 3rd January, 1879 Addison was instructed to obtain tenders for the construction of the line which was to be double track throughout. These were put before the committee on 6th May following :

	£	s.	d.
H. Lovatt	37,025	17	4
H. Harrison	39,220	0	0
Lucas & Aird	49,826	0	0
Wall Brothers	51,075	17	11
Engineer's estimate	38,540	17	2

The tender from Henry Lovatt of Wolverhampton was accepted, but he revised this downwards on 2nd June to £36,548 19s. 10d., which was approved and the contract was dated 27th June, 1879. Lovatt provided sureties totalling £750 by John Wilson, a farmer of Stoke Prior, Bromsgrove and Stratford Lovatt of 10 Aldermanbury, London. The latter was actually John Anthony Stratford Lovatt, and was Henry's brother trading at the given address as a cotton merchant. Specifically, the line was given as 2 miles 28.55 chains, and was to start from Aldridge at 10 chains north of a junction with the WWMJR. A penalty of £20 per day would be imposed for any unfinished work beyond the agreed completion date, which was given as 1st January, 1881. He was to commence work within 14 days of being possession of lands, and was responsible for determining if any mine workings were likely to cause subsidence, and for maintenance of the works for 12 months after completion. Monthly payments would be made, for up to 90 per cent of the contract value, as long as they were supported by the Engineer's certificates.

Ballast was to be of furnace cinders, and the MR was to provide permanent way materials, delivered to Aldridge. Seven bridges were required over or under roads, and at £16,613 2s. 3d. these proved to be the major cost of the line. Cuttings of 215,454 cubic yards and embankments of 122,370 cubic yards were to cost £12,119 5s. 9d., and laying of permanent way £6,088 9s. 10d. Some 10,010 linear yards of fencing totalled £1,376 7s. 6d. and culverts £351 14s. 6d.

Construction commenced immediately, and by 1st July, 1879, the committee approved the removal of excess permanent way material from the newly finished WWMJR, to Aldridge station for use on the new line. Surplus excavation from the Daw End Branch Canal at the northern end of Paul's Coppice was to be taken to Brownhills for the subsequent extension of the line across the Wyrley & Essington Canal there. As the line ran on an embankment for most of its length, this was a wise move.

By 2nd December, it was reported that difficulty was being experienced where the line passed through Walsall Wood Colliery, in depositing spoil and getting rid of surface water. A small diversion was suggested by Addison and approved by the committee.

Work had proceeded well by the following summer to the extent that Addison was considering the building of the station at Walsall Wood. He submitted plans on 1st June, 1880 for an island station, which was estimated to cost £3,051. However, the committee preferred his design of a two-platform station, which complete with buildings, waiting room, platforms and approaches was estimated at around £2,200. This cost was revised to £2,480 on 6th July, and Addison was instructed to invite tenders. The Traffic Department was to prepare plans and estimates for signalling the line.

On the afternoon of 20th June, the committee inspected the works. On 3rd August they were advised that the cost of telegraph for the branch would be £262 7s. 0d. At the next committee meeting, on 31st August, the tenders for the Walsall Wood station were examined:

	£	s.	d.
H.Lovatt	3,507	9	2
G. Lilley & Son	3,890	3	6
John Garlick	3,926	0	0
Jeffrey & Son	3,973	10	0
Wall Brothers	4,358	0	0
Engineer's estimate	3,312	2	2

Once again, Henry Lovatt had submitted the lowest bid, and was awarded the contract. Once more he revised his price downwards slightly (on 5th October) to £3,500 18s. 9d. which was also accepted. This was made up of:

	£	s.	d.
Station building	1,441	5	10
Waiting shed	429	13	0
Platforms	1,088	18	8
Fencing and gates	195	9	5
Weighhouse and machine pit	115	9	5
Cattle pens and dock	230	2	5
Total contract value	3,500	18	9

Conditions of the contract were similar to the first one above, and provided for a penalty payment of £20 per day for any work unfinished at the agreed completion date. This was to be four months from the date at which Lovatt was given possession of the lands. Payments to him would be made monthly, as long as they were supported by the Engineer's certificate of completed works and did not exceed 80 per cent of the contract value. Lovatt would be responsible for determining if any mines were likely to cause subsidence to buildings, and for the maintenance of all works for 12 months after completion.

The station building and the waiting shed were to be built in blue brick, with the latter having just one chimney. The awning from the station building over the platform was to be glazed. These were, in fact, the standard MR station buildings, as seen on the WWMJR line. It is interesting that no goods shed was specified here, and a simple 'lock-up' shed was eventually erected.

One month later, on 2nd November, 1880 it was noted that a siding had been put in up to the boundary of the Walsall Wood Colliery Co. 'for their accommodation'. However, there is no mention of the cost involved, and whether the MR or the colliery company was expected to pay for it.

It is not known for certain whether Henry Lovatt used any locomotives on the construction of this line, although it seems likely. It is suggested, but not confirmed, that he hired one locomotive from the Walsall Wood Colliery Company - a Beyer, Peacock 0-4-0ST (Works No. 1145 of 1872) named *Countess of Essex*, that had been acquired from an unknown source around 1881. This engine was supplied new to the contractor George Meakin & Son for use on the LNWR widening between Kings Langley and Willesden (1871 to 1875), but was afterwards put up for sale.

Construction was nearly complete early in 1881, as the committee requested the Locomotive Department to provide gas mains and fittings for the station at Walsall Wood, and for the Stores Department to supply a clock. On 3rd May the Locomotive Department was to supply the weighing machine for the goods yard. The committee were also informed on that date that the Government inspectors had approved the line, and that the MR Way & Works Department had taken the line under its charge from the preceding Saturday, 30th April.

There is no indication that traffic commenced immediately, although it seems likely that the MR and both the colliery owners at Aldridge and Walsall Wood would have been keen to see their output transported as soon as possible. Working timetables make no such mention, so it seems that such traffic, if any, would have been treated as being on a long siding from Aldridge to Walsall Wood, rather than as part of any through working as occurred after the completion of the entire line.

Nonetheless, there were still some issues with connections to local businesses, as on 4th April, 1882 a plan and estimate (£400) for a siding to be laid into the brick-making business of Joberns & Company at Aldridge was discussed by the Way & Works Committee, and referred to the General Purposes Committee, who approved it on 2nd May. However, the MR protected its investment by requiring the company to pay 3d. per ton for any deficiency if traffic was less than 5,000 tons annually.

Walsall Wood extension

Meanwhile, consideration had been given to an extension to Brownhills and beyond. Parliamentary approval for this line was included in a Bill presented for the 1880 session, which received Royal Assent on 6th August, 1880. This was the MR (Additional Powers) Act (Vict. 43 & 44, cap. 146), which in section 4 detailed Railway No. 5 as the 'Walsall Wood Branch Extension'. This was further spilt into two parts :

> *No. 1* - railway of 1 mile 1 furlong 6 chains 60 links from a junction with the Walsall Wood Branch 'now in construction' to a junction with the South Staffordshire Railway (actually the Norton Branch) of the LNWR at Norton Canes.
> *No. 2* – railway of 2 miles 7 chains at Norton Cross from a junction with railway No. 1 (above) to a junction with the railway of the CCWR Company.

The lines were to be double track, and five years were given for their completion. Railway No. 1 ran from the end of the Walsall Wood branch to Coppice Nos. 6 & 8 pits at Wilkin and thence to the LNWR Norton branch. Railway No. 2 ran from this line near to the southern part of Chasewater (just north of the present day headquarters of the Chasewater Railway) to join the CCWR at a point which later became known as MR Cannock Chase although certain LMS notices referred to it also as Brownhills Conduit Colliery sidings. This gave the company an important link to Conduit Colliery, and to other pits linked to the CCWR.

The General Purposes Committee was notified on 5th October, 1880 that the MR Board, in their Minute No. 2508, had required them to proceed with obtaining plans, sections and tenders for the extension. This committee seems to have taken over the role of supervising the construction of the extension, and so reviewed the plans at this meeting.

Tenders were examined by the committee on 31st March, 1881:

	£	s.	d.
J. Garlick	40,816	7	3
T. Horsman & Co.	41,157	11	11
H. Lovatt	42,755	0	2
J. & G. Tomlinson	43,205	11	2
Killett & Bentley	43,436	18	4
W. Mousley	43,988	2	3
Logan & Hemingway	47,652	18	0
W. Rigby	48,190	4	7
Engineer's estimate	47,799	8	11

Being the lowest, John Garlick's tender was accepted, although a small error was noted and this was later revised downwards by 1s. 8d!

The minutes of this committee give little detail as to the progress with construction, which therefore is presumed to have proceeded without any problems. On 2nd January, 1883 the committee was informed that siding accommodation for Coppice Colliery would cost an estimated £1,480. This matter was referred to the General Purposes Committee, who approved the plan and expenditure on 1st February. On 30th April next, the line was said to be shortly ready for passenger traffic, and the Way & Works Department took over the line the following day.

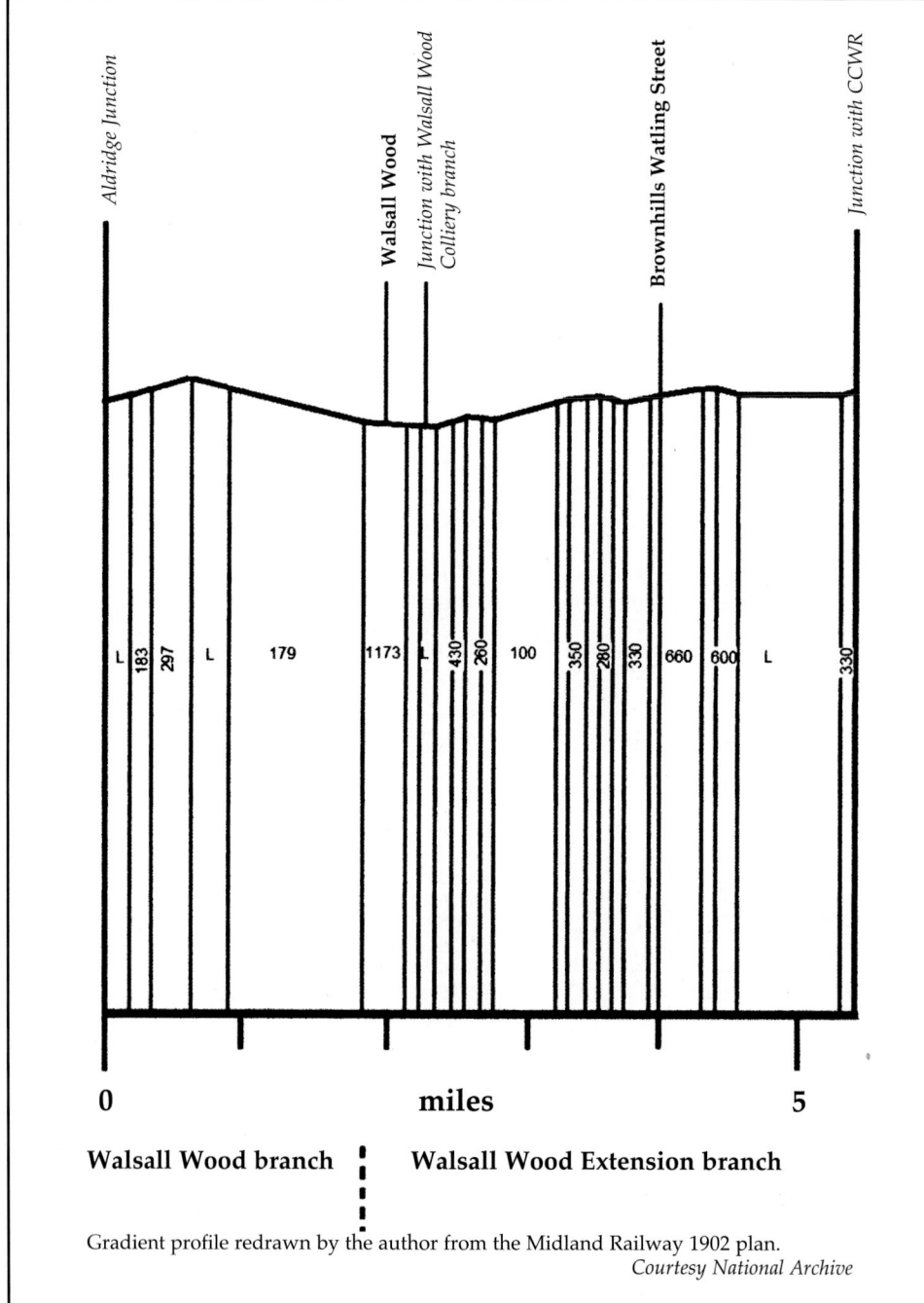

Gradient profile redrawn by the author from the Midland Railway 1902 plan.
Courtesy National Archive

Opening

The line from Aldridge to Brownhills was opened to 'goods traffic' as from 1st April, 1882, and was worked by block telegraph from this date. The line through from Brownhills to Cannock Chase was opened for mineral traffic from 1st November, 1882. However, the goods facilities at Walsall Wood and Brownhills are recorded as being ready to accept traffic only in July 1883, so the assumption is that 'open for goods' may have meant that colliery traffic was using the line from these dates in 1882, and that general merchandise was only handled from July 1883.

Passenger working began on Tuesday 1st July, 1884. This was recorded in the *Walsall Observer and South Staffordshire Chronicle* of 28th June, 1884 as follows:

> The Midland Railway Guide for July contains an announcement that the recently-constructed line from Aldridge to Brownhills, passing through Walsall Wood, will be opened on Tuesday next. As an experiment, there is to be a service of three trains a day each way, with an extra market train on Saturday nights. No doubt they are arranged to meet those passing both ways at Aldridge, thus affording additional accommodation for people in the district mentioned to get to Sutton, Birmingham, Walsall, and, in fact, the whole of the Midland system. The opening of this line has been looked forward to with considerable interest, especially by the inhabitants of the Old Watling Street, at Brownhills, to whom it will be a great boon. The line extends beyond Brownhills, but the section mentioned is all that is to be opened for passenger traffic at present.

There is no suggestion of garlands decorating the line, nor of sumptuous meals being devoured by the contractors and Directors, as occurred with earlier railways. By this date, new railways were no longer an excuse for such outlandish celebration; they were considered as essential to the prosperity of any area, and as such, simply another amenity.

A very early photograph of Brownhills MR station, looking north. This must have been taken shortly after opening in 1882, as the platforms and buildings appear pristine. Notable are the ornate chimneys and barge boards of the main station building. In the background there appears to be two passenger carriages, probably awaiting their next turn along the line to Aldridge.   *Bill Mayo Collection*

A flooded Walsall Wood station viewed from the Lichfield Road bridge, looking towards Brownhills some time in the late 1920s. The station was evidently still in use at this time, although rail services would have been temporarily suspended. Goods wagons are stabled in the yard at the rear of the up platform.
Bill Mayo Collection

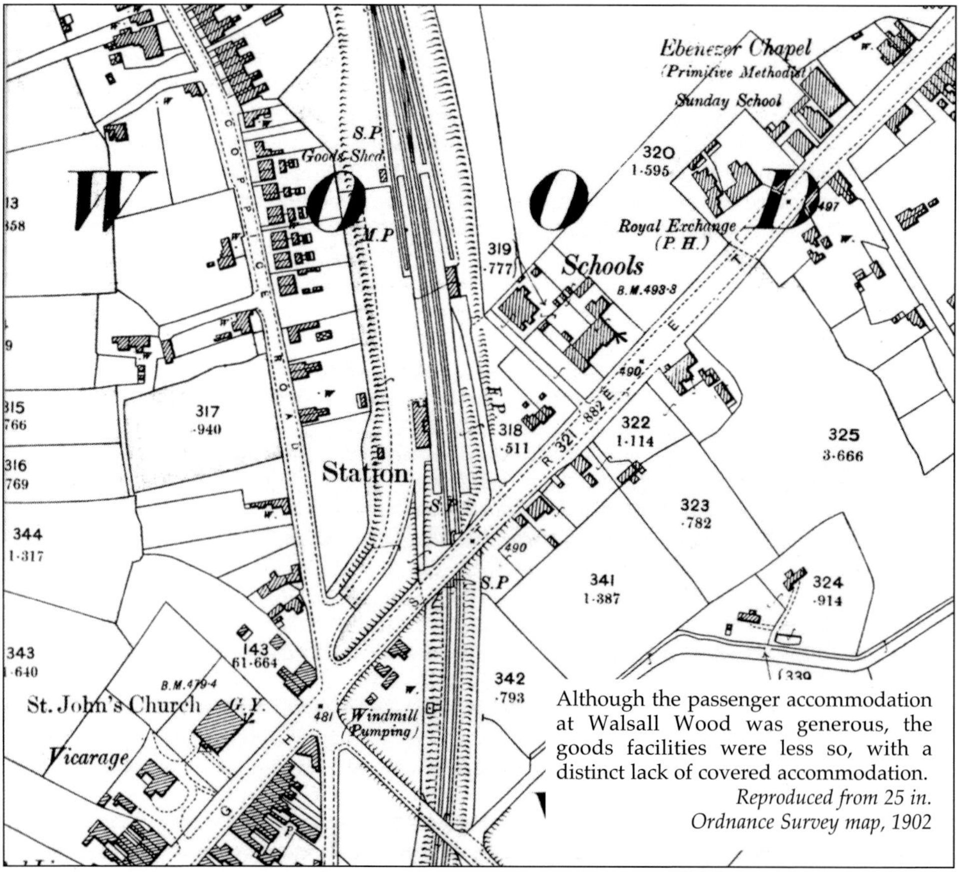

Although the passenger accommodation at Walsall Wood was generous, the goods facilities were less so, with a distinct lack of covered accommodation.
Reproduced from 25 in. Ordnance Survey map, 1902

Description of the line

Starting at Aldridge, the line curved away northwards at a junction with the WWMJR line, almost immediately throwing off the lines to the goods yard described in Chapter Five. Opposite on the left a connection had once been made to the Victoria Colliery, but this mine closed in 1889 and the connection was removed shortly afterwards. Beyond here the line straightened to a northerly direction, passed over Middlemore Lane and then Leighswood Lane, shortly passing Leighswood Colliery on the left, but making no connection. A short distance further on a siding gave connection (1 mile from Aldridge) to the Aldridge Colliery Co. on the left, which after the closure of the colliery in 1930 concentrated on the production of bricks and tiles. The company used narrow gauge tramways in and around its works and to connect to the nearby Daw End Branch Canal. One tramway, of the unusual gauge of 2 ft 2½ in. was used to haul marl from its own pit to the works. Although the works was also connected to the LNWR Leighswood branch, it never employed its own standard gauge locomotives, relying on the MR or LNWR to work the appropriate and quite extensive sidings.

Still running on an embankment, about ¼ mile further on the line passed beneath Coppy (or Coppice) Lane and then a connection was made (at 1½ mile) from a junction on the up line only, to a siding of around 150 yards in length serving the Coppice Lane Tileries of Joseph Joberns & Co. Once again this company used a narrow gauge tramway, linking to its quarry, and also alongside Coppy Lane to a wharf on the canal. Since leaving Aldridge the line had been climbing, although at nothing steeper than 1 in 297. After a short level stretch, the line passed through a small area of farming countryside and began a gradual descent at a steady 1 in 179 all the way to **Walsall Wood** (2 miles), where the line was virtually level. The station buildings here were immediately to the north of the Lichfield Road bridge which passed over the line, and were of the standard MR brick-built type, as described in the Chapter Five. An approach road led from Coppice Road almost at its junction with Lichfield Road, to the station buildings on the down side. A footpath also led from Lichfield Road to the up platform. A single siding was provided on the down side, accessed via a backshunt from the down running line, north of the station, and a small 'lock-up' goods shed (not rail served) was eventually constructed. On the up side, the single line from Walsall Wood Colliery joined the running line, just as it passed beneath the northern end of Coppice Road, north of the station. But it also continued southwards towards the station, diverging into one double-ended loop line and one single-ended siding. The loop line joined the down running line north of the station, with a short refuge siding terminating at the northern platform end. The single-ended siding continued further, into the goods yard at the rear of the down platform, where another small goods lock-up was situated.

After about 120 yards, the connection into Walsall Wood Colliery split into two, with the left-hand line itself further splitting into one siding which ran to a canal wharf and one eventually feeding two groups of a total of eight double-ended sidings that passed beneath the screens. Meanwhile, the right-hand line also split

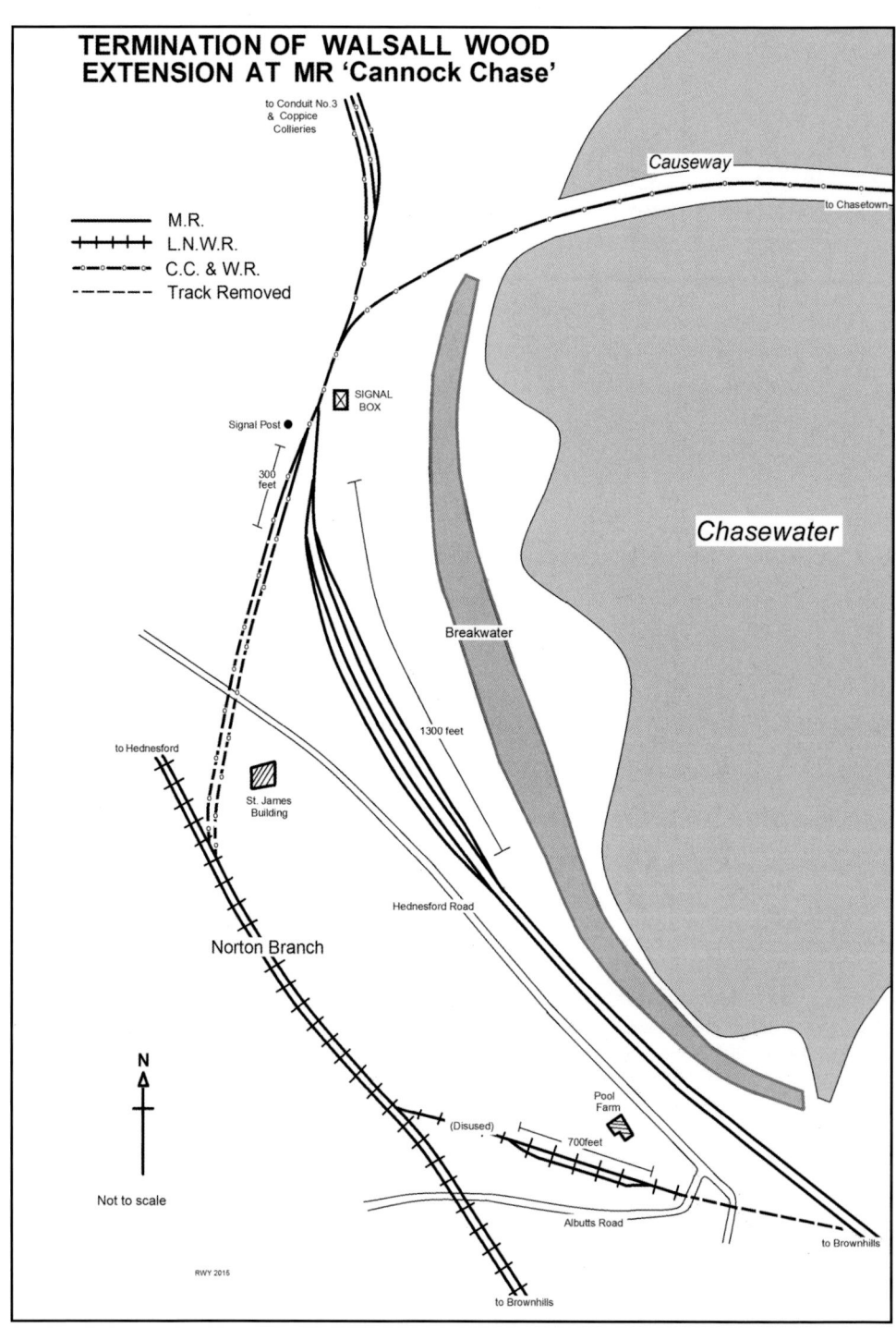

into two, with one becoming a group of three double-ended marshalling sidings and the other running to the company's brick works. At the north end of all of these four groups of sidings, they once again joined together to form the LNWR running line that joined the South Staffordshire line at Norton Junction. In this way the colliery enjoyed access to both the LNWR and MR systems. Details of the locomotives used at the colliery are given in *Appendix One*.

Returning to the Brownhills branch, after passing under the northern end of Coppice Road it almost immediately crossed over the BCN Daw End Branch Canal, which then gradually swung away north-eastwards. Still on an embankment and now climbing at 1 in 100, the line passed over the LNWR branch to Walsall Wood Colliery and through Clayhanger Common, crossing Bridge Street in the middle of the common. This had been common land for many centuries, but was eventually enclosed by 1876, although the area was still known as Clayhanger Common. Continuing on the embankment, the line then crossed, in fairly quick succession, firstly the Wyrley and Essington Canal then the LNWR South Staffordshire line from Walsall to Lichfield, then Pelsall Road (now A4124), climbing at an easy pace of no more than 1 in 220. The view changed somewhat as it passed through a heavily wooded area, and then across the Chester Road (A452) into **Brownhills** station (4 miles). This was situated alongside Chester Road and actually on Brownhills Common. The station buildings once again conformed to the standard MR style as described for Aldridge, and were situated on the up side, with a small waiting room positioned in the centre of the down platform. Road access to the station and goods yard was from Chester Road, and a footpath also led to the down platform. The goods yard comprised a single lengthy loop on the up side, north of the station, from which two widely spaced sidings were sited in the yard to the east. A small goods shed was positioned alongside one of the sidings. A further short siding led to a side- and end-loading dock, at the north end of the up platform. A crossover was positioned at the north end of the shunting neck, to permit down trains to enter the yard, and was actually sited beneath the road bridge carrying the Watling Street (A5) over the line.

As the line continued northwards it swung slightly to the north-west, continuing on an embankment and dropping at a casual 1 in 220/330 until it reached the junction for the line to Wilkin. This line curved off, as a single line to the west, passing beneath Hednesford Road, then over Albutts Road before reaching the exchange sidings for Coppice No. 6 and 8 pits. Beyond these 700 ft-long sidings, it turned north-westwards to make a single connection with the LNWR Norton branch.

Meanwhile, the line to Cannock Chase reached a level section for about ½ mile as it travelled on another embankment, with fine views of Chasewater to the right, until it reached the Cannock Chase exchange sidings (5½ miles). These comprised two loops, one for each running line, of around ¼ mile which terminated at the junction with the single line CCWR. A signal box under the control of the CCWR was sited at this junction. Here the CCWR line to Chasetown forked off to the right, whilst a left-hand line ran to Conduit Colliery and was the property of that company. Further to the left, the CCWR originally ran from 1867 to a double track connection with the LNWR Norton branch, but this connection was removed around 1884 and the line thereafter truncated to form two lengthy sidings.

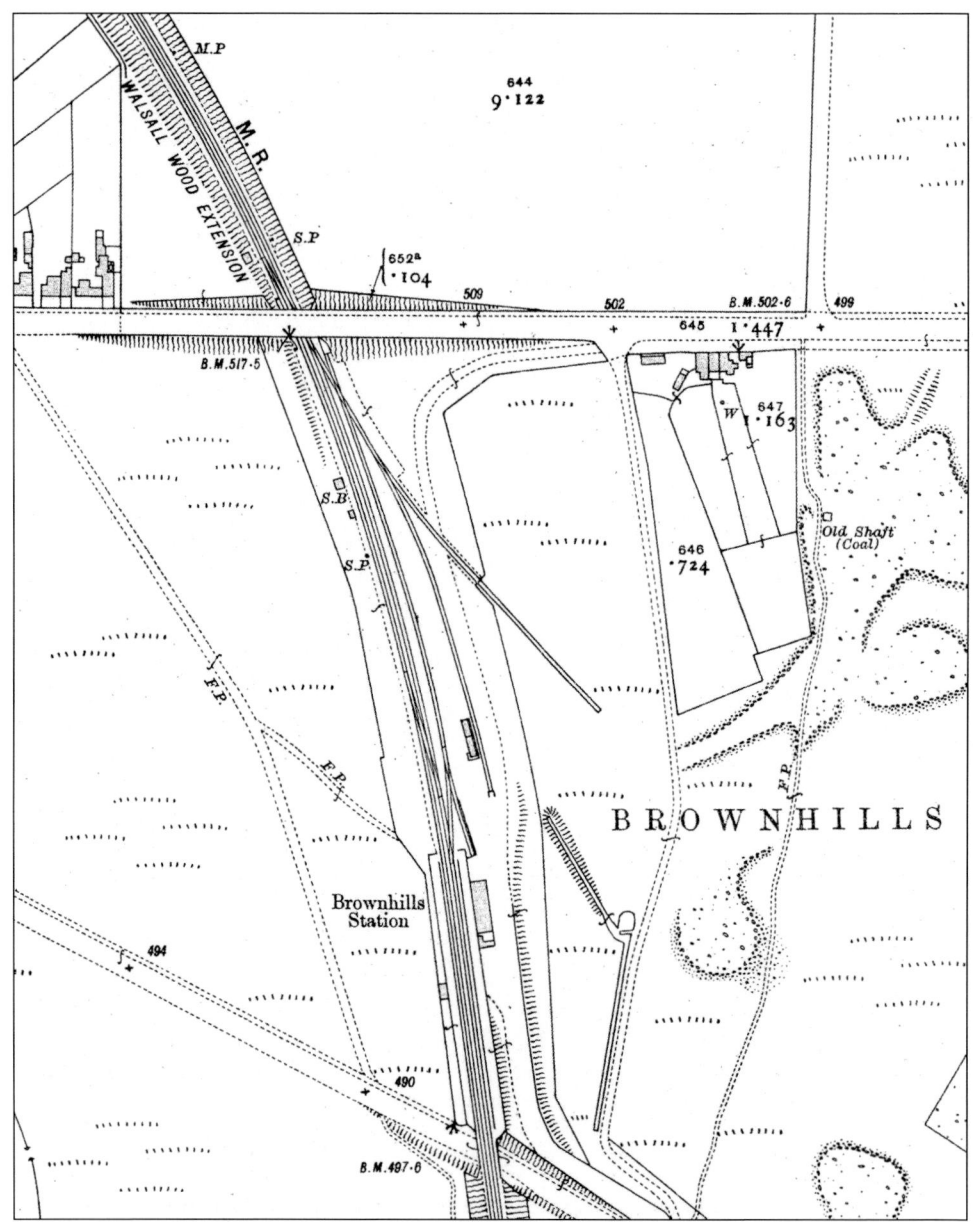

Brownhills station and goods yard was situated on Brownhills Common, between the A452 Chester Road North (lower road) and the A5 Watling Street (upper). Evidence of mining activity in the area is clear.
Reproduced from 25 in. Ordnance Survey map, 1919

Passenger services

The *Walsall Observer and South Staffordshire Chronicle* listed the opening services in its edition of 5th July, 1884. Trains only ran between Brownhills and Aldridge with the one intermediate stop at Walsall Wood, at 8.05 am, 1.35 and 6.55 pm, with a further Saturdays-only market day service at 8.50 pm. In the reverse direction, trains left Aldridge at 8.47 am, 2.07 and 7.22 pm, and the market day train returned at 10.00 pm. There were never any Sunday trains on this line. The duration of each journey took between 13 and 15 minutes. It will be noted that the first train each day started from Brownhills, where the carriage(s) were stabled overnight. The locomotive ran as light engine to or from Cannock Chase to continue with coal traffic.

This timetable continued unchanged until 1906 by which time an additional Saturday train had been inserted, and times changed a little; departures from Brownhills were at 7.55 am, 1.25, 4.25 (SO), 6.42, 9.15 pm (SO) and from Aldridge at 8.35 am, 2.16, 4.57 (SO), 7.30 and 10.38 pm (SO).

The times were similar in 1912, but three years later during World War I the last train of the day on Saturdays had been withdrawn. By May 1920 the service had shrunk again, to just two daily, and now ran from Brownhills at 7.52 am, 1.09 (SO), and 5.57 pm (SX), returning from Aldridge at 8.30 am, 2.12 (SO) and 7.40 pm (SX). Thus anyone wishing to travel to Aldridge for the market and then enjoy an evening in that town (or even further afield, perhaps Walsall) could no longer do so, as there was no late evening train to return on.

In July of the following year, the service still only comprised two daily trains each way, but the times had changed again : Brownhills depart at 7.52 am, 4.20 (SO), 5.57 pm (SX); Aldridge depart 8.30 am, 6.45 (SO), 8.18 pm (SX). So passengers could once again spend a little time at the market. The same service operated in 1922, and there were no further changes until the cessation of passenger services.

Following the Grouping in 1923, Brownhills station was renamed Brownhills Watling Street on 2nd June, 1924 to distinguish it from its neighbour, the LNWR station on the SSR Walsall-Lichfield line, which on the same day was also renamed, this time as Brownhills High Street. Passenger services were withdrawn as from 31st March, 1930, with Brownhills Watling Street station closing entirely, but somewhat surprisingly Walsall Wood remained open for goods.

A final consideration should be given to the provision of two platforms at Walsall Wood and Brownhills. As a rather sparse service was offered right from the beginning, it may be thought that this was an extravagance, and that simple single platform stations would have sufficed. That is certainly true concerning the number of passengers involved. However, the line had been built as double track, with the evident expectation of considerable mineral traffic. It would therefore have been rather difficult to cater for passengers on a single platform, whilst operating a double track system. This would otherwise have involved complex pointwork and interlocking, as well as difficult operations in switching trains from one line to another - so providing an extra platform was almost certainly the cheaper option at that time.

A rather large party of schoolchildren at Brownhills station awaiting their train for a day out, probably to Tamworth Castle or Dudley Castle, as these were popular local destinations. Many of the children can be seen to be clutching their sandwiches, in preparation for a picnic. The date is likely to be in the 1920s.
Bill Mayo Collection

A posed photograph of the MR station at Brownhills with Fowler LMS 0-6-0 No. 3690 having arrived with a two-coach passenger train, sometime in the late 1920s. This engine had been built by Johnson in 1901 as one his numerous class '1873', but was rebuilt by Fowler with a larger boiler in 1923. There appears to be full turnout of the station staff and engine crew for the photograph. The generous layout of the facilities can be appreciated. *Lens of Sutton/R.C. Carpenter*

Fowler 0-6-0 No. 3277 (originally a Johnson '1873' class engine) standing in the station at Brownhills with what is believed to be the last train prior to closure. This was the 4.20 pm (SO) to Aldridge on 29th March, 1930. The driver is obviously expecting rain, as he has partially unfurled the weather tarpaulin on the cab roof. The wooden construction of the platform on the down side is evident in the foreground. *Author's Collection*

Another view of the last train from Brownhills to Aldridge on 29th March, 1930. The station porter is holding up some sort of a notice, possibly to commemorate the event. In this view, it may be seen that the nearest coach is a 12-wheel saloon. The vehicle next to No. 3277 features a clerestory roof. *Author's Collection*

Walsall Wood station was just about still standing (although partly roofless) in 1947 when this photograph was taken. The unused up platform is on the right, having been abandoned since closure 17 years earlier. Nevertheless, coal traffic was still plentiful, as can be seen from the rows of wagons in the distance towards Walsall Wood pit. *Author's Collection*

The SLS special of 26th May, 1951 formed of Ivatt class '2' 2-6-2T No. 41226 sandwiched between two 2-coach auto-trains visited the Brownhills branch. It is seen here crossing the Chester Road near to Brownhills station. In the centre is an advert for Mitchells & Butler's Export Ale, an example of another long lost brewery. *Author's Collection*

The 1951 SLS special paused at the site of Brownhills station before retracing its tracks back to Aldridge, and continuing the tour. The site of the platforms is alongside the engine and furthest two coaches. *Author's Collection*

The 1959 SLS special continued along the former Walsall Wood branch as far as the Cannock Chase exchange sidings near to Chasewater, which is off to the left. In this view the special has reached the permitted extent of the line, and once again, participants detrain to examine and photograph the area. *Transport Treasury/A.E. Bennett*

The derelict station at Walsall Wood on 30th May, 1959 as an SLS special consisting of two three-car Metro-Cammell dmus pulls into the station. The station and the siding seems to be used for storing redundant permanent way materials, mostly sleepers. *R.S. Carpenter Collection*

Goods services

Further sidings for the important coal traffic were put in after the opening. On 20th March, 1884 the General Purposes Committee approved the installation of additional sidings at Walsall Wood Colliery at a cost of £250. On 15th May that year, this committee approved expenditure of £1,020 for sidings at Aldridge Colliery.

Goods services also only ever ran on Mondays to Saturdays, and can be summarized as follows:

	Feb. 1883	Oct. 1890	Jul. 1906	May 1920	Jul. 1939	Jun.-Sep. 1958
Empty to Cannock Chase	2	4+2 MThX +1 as required	3	3	2	1+2 SX
Empty to Walsall Wood	1	0	0	0	incl.	incl.
Empty to Brownhills	0	1	2	0	0	0
Empty to Aldridge Colliery/Brickworks	0	0	1	0	incl.	1
Minerals from Cannock Chase	2	1+2 MThX +1 as required	4	4	2	1+ 2SX
Minerals from Walsall Wood	1	0	0	0	incl.	incl.
Minerals from Brownhills	0	1	1	0	0	0
Minerals/goods from Aldridge Colliery/Brickworks	0	0	incl.	1	incl.	1

All of the workings are described as mineral or empty mineral, indicating a distinct lack of general goods traffic. It seems unlikely that there was none at all, so the only conclusion is that such traffic was attached to the mineral workings - or, indeed, the passenger workings up to 1930.

It will be seen that the most important traffic was from the CCWR connection at Cannock Chase, and a further amount from Walsall Wood Colliery. During this period, at least three of the workings each way went through to Birmingham, usually to Lawley Street goods yard. By 1939 services had been curtailed somewhat, so that Walsall Wood and Aldridge Collieries were not served separately, the 'incl.' above denoting that the Cannock Chase trains called there. Also at this time, only one daily coal train then ran from Aldridge, terminating at Washwood Heath. The balancing empties working originated from Camp Hill Goods in Birmingham. All other colliery traffic from the branch was dealt with at Aldridge by passing local freights. The reality of this apparent decline in traffic is not due to any reduction in outputs at the collieries, simply that the traffic was carried on other routes across the Chase, with the notable exception of Aldridge Colliery.

Over the years it is not surprising that the colliery workings in this district may have caused subsidences that may have affected the line to some degree or another. A careful watch was necessary to ensure that any signs were immediately investigated, and corrected as far as possible, in order to avoid accidents through derailments. Even as early as 1883 the MR Way & Works Committee was being advised that supports may be necessary for Brownhills station.

The short line from north of Brownhills that gave access to the colliery at Wilkin had only opened in 1884, but the colliery closed in 1894, and this line was reported to have been taken up at that time. However, the Ordnance Survey map for 1901 still shows the line in place, although as 'disused'.

Curiously, the branch had survived World War I without being singled at any point, unlike the more significant lines of the WWR and WWMJR. However, this was not to last, for the section between Brownhills and Cannock Chase was singled with effect from 13th January, 1924, this then being worked by train staff without tickets. Brownhills signal box also closed with the cessation of passenger services on 31st March, 1930. The remaining section (Aldridge to Brownhills) was thereafter worked as 'one engine in steam'. On 25th March, 1932 the signal box at Walsall Wood was burned down, and was presumably replaced by a ground frame, although this is not certain.

However, the 1937 LMS Sectional Appendix noted that 'the up line (southbound) between Conduit Colliery Sidings and Walsall Wood Station is blocked with wagons' and that therefore both up and down trains must use the down running line between these two points. Note that the sidings at 'Cannock Chase had by this time become known as Conduit Colliery Sidings'.

At Aldridge, the section from the goods yard to Aldridge Colliery was singled as from 30th June, 1940 as a wartime economy measure, and the next section onwards to Walsall Wood was also singled, from 7th July, 1940. It is presumed that the wagons stored in 1937 on the up line had by then been removed. The signal box at Aldridge Colliery remained until 3rd March, 1946 when it was taken out of use, although it can have seen little use during the war. It was replaced by two ground frames (one at the north end, and one at the south end).

The line was officially closed as from 23rd March, 1957 from a point near to Brownhills station site and just on the north side of the A5 Watling Street, for ¾ mile northwards to the Conduit Colliery sidings. However, the 1958 working timetable still showed workings to Conduit Colliery sidings, so evidently this closure was not carried out right away. As the section from Brownhills to Walsall Wood Colliery was not closed until some time around September 1960, it may be that the rails on this northernmost section remained until that time. The remainder of the branch was closed as from 2nd August, 1965, and became an extended siding into the BICC works at Aldridge from that date, although the track as far as Walsall Wood remained *in situ* for a number of years. The BICC works were situated alongside Brickyard Lane near to its junction with Northgate Way, and so this extended siding ran for about ⅞ mile. The works constructed the masts for the electrification of lines throughout the West Midlands at the time. The preformed masts were taken out by rail, usually on a Friday for installation at the required sites over the weekend. Brian Cresswell, who worked there at the time, can also remember occasions when some incoming wagons were given a rough shunt, and travelled uncontrolled along the closed section almost into Walsall Wood. Retrieval of the runaway wagons was often a protracted affair. Finally, with the completion of electrification works in this area, the BICC siding closed on 9th February, 1969, and the remaining section to Aldridge Junction closed the following day.

The line was worked by block telegraph from its opening in 1882 until the singling of the line in 1924 northwards from Brownhills. From 31st March, 1930 the whole line north from Aldridge Colliery Sidings was worked under the 'one engine in steam' regulations until closure. In fact, the final short section from Aldridge Junction to these sidings was eventually also believed to have been classed as 'one engine in steam', although it is not known when this came into force.

Locomotives in use on the line are believed to have been exclusively 0-6-0s ranging from the Johnson varieties to those of Fowler's LMS '3F' and '4F' classes, and were used on both passenger and goods duties. In the latter years, such workings as did appear were likely to have been powered by class '20', '25' or '31' diesels.

There was a single speed limit for the whole branch of 30 mph, with 15 mph over the junction at Aldridge with the WWMJR line.

Only one accident is known to have occurred, and this in the line's final years. It was reported in the *Railway Observer* of October 1961 as follows:

> MR branch from Aldridge through Brownhills to Conduit Colliery opened in 1882, has been lifted beyond Walsall Wood Colliery. This colliery is scheduled to be closed next year and the fate of the remainder of the line is in doubt. On 27th August 1961 Class 4F 44333 returning from Walsall Wood Colliery with 11 wagons was derailed and plunged down the embankment due to some boys putting an inverted rail chair on the track. The crew escaped serious injury and the locomotive did not appear to be badly damaged.

A search of local newspapers has failed to find any further details of this accident, and what action was taken against the boys, or even if they were traced.

Railtour visits to this line were infrequent, and details of those which occurred on 26th May, 1951 and 23rd March, 1963 may be found in Chapter Five.

This photograph of Coppice (or 'Coppy') Pit was taken from the colliery spoil heap during the 1920s and viewed towards the south-east. Numerous narrow gauge mine wagons are visible in the centre of the picture, and standard gauge coal wagons are marshalled towards the screens. The road leading uphill off to the left centre is Ingles Road (now Brownhills Road). *Bill Mayo Collection*

The West Midlands leg of 'The Gwent Growler' railtour of 14th April, 1990 ran from Wolverhampton via Walsall, Park Lane Junction, Castle Bromwich, and the Camp Hill line to Cheltenham and Gloucester. Here it is seen passing through the remains of Sutton Park station behind English Electric class '37' Co-Co locomotives Nos. 37254 and 37073. The line through the goods shed was still extant at this time. *R. Monk*

In connection with an open day at Bescot traction maintenance depot on 6th May, 1990, a dmu shuttle service was run between Birmingham New Street and Walsall via the Sutton Park route, calling at Bescot for visitors. On this occasion, Tyseley's Metropolitan-Cammell class '101' set No. T409 has left Walsall and is seen passing Eastview Road, Sutton Coldfield. It appears to have been strengthened by the addition of a further single car unit. *R. Monk*

Chapter Nine

Recent times

It almost goes without saying that as the first closure of a part of the WWR and the withdrawal of passenger services on the WWMJR was over 40 years ago, much of the infrastructure will have disappeared.

Starting at the Wolverhampton end of the line, a couple of hundred yards of track remain heading eastwards from what was Heath Town Junction and the earthworks of the line do remain, still passing on underline girder bridges over what were Inkerman Street, Alma Street and Grove Street. However, these streets have been truncated and traffic no longer actually passes beneath the bridges. But the line down to the GWR at Low Level station, and the entire site of Wednesfield Road goods depot and yard have been redeveloped as part of a new Royal Mail sorting centre. The site of the Canal goods depot was similarly incorporated into that of the latter Corus Steel Stockholding site, now itself closed and the site once more idle.

Continuing eastwards the bridge abutments at Deans Road still remain, pointing the way east, but beyond here the route of the railway has been taken over by commercial development and a new road 'Wednesfield Way' (A4124), which bypasses Wednesfield town centre. The site of Wednesfield station is buried beneath this new road. Beyond here the line of the railway disappears, due mainly to housing development in the Little London area, until the outskirts of the town centre of Willenhall. Nothing remains of the station, and the former goods yard has been leveled and now forms part of the park. However, the deep cutting where the station once stood is clearly visible, and forms a footpath from near the Memorial Park through the northern edge of the town, burrowing beneath Temple Bar and Cemetery Road. Overline bridges at these roads remain in good order.

Continuing eastwards the line then runs on an embankment at the rear of several small factories. At the crossing of Annes Road, the underline bridge has been completely removed, but the embankment continues on the other side, crossing Stringes (or Stringers) Lane then over the course of the Bentley Canal, although once again the bridges have been removed.

As it continues eastwards, the course of the line is partially visible, but it has been encroached upon by some commercial businesses between Charles Street and Clarke's Lane in Ashmore Lake. The bridge over Clarke's Lane also has been completely removed and a new fire station erected on the former gas works site. Again, nothing remains of Short Heath station. Eastwards from here the area has been taken up with new housing, but the trackbed remains, mostly on a small embankment and in use as a 'linear park' all the way through Bentley and to where the M6 bisects the route. Bentley station site is below the surface of the northbound lanes of the M6 motorway.

East of the M6 the trackbed is more easily traceable, on the north side of Reedswood Way, where an overline bridge remains intact, and another as it passes beneath Green Lane, Walsall (A34) and reaches North Walsall. The

In the afternoon of 6th May, 1990, the second leg of 'The Ironbridge Rambler', running as 1T57, traversed the WWMJR with fresh motive power in the form of class '20s' Nos. 20143 and 20130. In this view it is approaching the remains of Sutton Park station, where the up platform can still be seen, even if somewhat overgrown. *R. Monk*

On 16th July, 1990, two English Electric class '20' Bo-Bos Nos. 20025 and 20096 were bound for Bescot with a haul of ballast hoppers, but made an enforced stop on the WWMJR at Eastview Road, Sutton Coldfield when smoke began billowing from the second locomotive. The cause was eventually diagnosed as sticking brakes, and after isolating them the train continued its journey. *R. Monk*

Sulzer class '47' Co-Co No. 47359 passes Sutton Park on 17th September, 1990 with a train of empty carflats, almost certainly bound for Washwood Heath Sidings. *R. Monk*

Doncaster-built class '58' Co-Co No. 58009 with a track panel train, running 'wrong line' due to an engineering possession at Eastview Road, Sutton Coldfield on 3rd February, 1991. Newly installed track can be seen in the foreground. *R. Monk*

Two track-laying machines busy at work replacing track panels on the WWMJR near Sutton Coldfield on 3rd February, 1991. The road in the background is Eastview Road, along which steel 'security fencing' has since been installed, thus severely limiting photographic opportunities at this point. *R. Monk*

Further permanent way work was necessary at the Eastview Road cutting on 10th May, 1992, with class '47' No. 47376 *Skylark* seen here in charge of a train dropping ballast from hoppers on to the formation. *R. Monk*

BR Standard class '8P' 4-6-2 No. 71000 *Duke of Gloucester* makes a fine sight as it passes the abandoned Sutton Park station on 28th August, 1992. The 'Bescot Century Limited' headboard is a bit misleading, as it was hauling just three support coaches. At Bescot two days later, this locomotive provided shuttle train rides within the confines of Bescot sidings, topped and tailed with BR class '7P' Pacific No. 70000 *Britannia*. *R. Monk*

Doncaster built Co-Co No. 56071 passes through Sutton Coldfield with a coal train consisting of HAA wagons, almost certainly from Daw Mill Colliery in Warwickshire, and bound for either of the power stations at Ironbridge or Rugeley. The date is 22nd June, 1995. *R. Monk*

General Electric Co-Co No. 66042 passes through Sutton Coldfield with a coal train consisting of HAA wagons, probably from Daw Mill Colliery in Warwickshire, and once again bound for either Ironbridge or Rugeley power stations. The date is 23rd May, 2001. *R. Monk*

Park Lane Junction is difficult to photograph, being hemmed in by industrial premises and located on an embankment. This ground level shot shows Hawksworth '94XX' 0-6-0PT No. 9466 having just passed over the junction, and crossing Park Lane, with a rail tour from Tyseley to Ironbridge on 3rd November, 2007. *Author*

bridge over the line carrying Bloxwich Road (B4210) is still extant, and the cutting here is extremely overgrown, so there are no remains of the station, closed in 1925. The bridge abutments of the line across the Cannock line and the SSR Lichfield line have even been removed. But, of course, the line from Ryecroft through to Water Orton remains in use, although all trace of the stations at Aldridge, Streetly, Sutton Park and Penns have gone. The surprising exception is that Sutton Town station building remains, although minus its platforms, and today is kept in immaculate condition as commercial premises. However, the original goods shed at Sutton Park remains, although seemingly almost derelict. The adjacent premises of the Royal Mail sorting depot are, of course, no longer rail served, but still perform the original function.

On the Brownhills branch, so much commercial development has occurred in the Aldridge, Walsall Wood and Brownhills area that it is quite surprising to find that the course of the railway can be traced. At Middlemore Lane in Aldridge the underline bridge has been removed along with the embankment on the north side, but that on the south side remains. At Walsall Wood the brickworks once occupied by the Joberns Company still produces bricks, but in a modern building and now owned by Ibstock plc. Overline bridges with blue-brick abutments and steelplate girders at Vigo Lane and Coppice Lane are still *in situ*, and at Lichfield Road (A461) it is just possible to trace earthworks for the rail alignment, confirming the site of Walsall Wood station here. A short distance further on, at Coppice Road earthworks can be discerned, as at Bridge Street in Brownhills. At the crossing point of the Chester Road (A452) in Brownhills the lower part of the bridge abutment on the eastern side remains, so fixing the site of Brownhills MR station. The point at which the line passed beneath the A5 is difficult to spot, due to making the A5 a dual carriageway here, with the consequent levelling. And to the north of the crossing lies the M6 Toll road which has obliterated any trace of the line. But immediately to the north of this motorway, the Chasewater Railway runs on the formation of the line to its finality, and indeed beyond on the tracks of the CCWR to Chasetown.

Nothing can be found of the short branch to Coppice No. 6 and No. 8 pits at Wilkin.

Tyseley's GWR 'Castle' class 4-6-0 No. 5029 *Nunney Castle* climbs westwards through Eastview Road cutting on a rather dull 28th April, 2008 with 'The City of Chester' railtour from Tyseley to Chester. This locomotive worked the return leg back to Tyseley later that day. *R. Monk*

Appendix One

Industrial locomotives

Locomotives known to have worked on the industrial standard gauge lines in the area are listed below. To identify the type of locomotive the wheel arrangement has been shown in the usual fashion for steam locomotives. Locomotives whose driving wheels are connected by rods are shown as 0-4-0D, etc. Those whose wheels are driven by chains or motors are as shown as 4w (4 wheel). These abbreviations for type have also been used:

Crane	Self propelled crane
DE	Diesel-electric
DH	Diesel-hydraulic
DM	Diesel-mechanical
ST	Saddle tank
T	Tank engine

The following abbreviations for locomotive builders have been used:

AB	Andrew Barclay, Sons & Co. Ltd, Kilmarnock
BP	Beyer, Peacock & Co. Ltd, Manchester
Crewe	LNWR, Crewe Works
Chasetown	Cannock Chase Colliery Co. Ltd, Chasetown Workshops
Derby	BR, Derby Works
HC	Hudswell, Clarke & Co. Ltd, Leeds
HE	Hunslet Engine Co. Ltd, Leeds
HL	R. & W. Hawthorn, Leslie & Co. Ltd, Newcastle-upon-Tyne
JS	John Smith, Coven, Staffs
K	Kitson & Co. Ltd, Leeds
Lill	Lilleshall Co. Ltd, Oakengates, Shropshire
MW	Manning, Wardle & Co. Ltd, Leeds
P	Peckett & Sons Ltd, Bristol
RH	Ruston & Hornsby Ltd, Lincoln
SB	Sharp Brothers & Co., Manchester
TSmith	Thos Smith & Sons (Rodley) Ltd, Rodley, Leeds
YE	Yorkshire Engine Co. Ltd., Sheffield

From Wolverhampton to Walsall

Engine No./name	Type	Cyl.	Builder	Works No. & date	Dates on site
British Steel Corporation (later Rotherham Engineering Steels Ltd), Wolverhampton					
	4w crane		T. Smith		1970-71
Elizabeth	0-4-0DE		YE	2506/1952	c.3/1971-1/1973
	4wDM		RH	402812/1957	c.11/1971-c.9/1975
Stanton No. 45	0-4-0DE		YE	2623/1956	c.9/1974-c.1992
10 *George*	0-4-0DE		YE	2797/1960	7/1982-c.1989

YE 2623 lost its coupling rods and was used as a 2w-2DE. External rail traffic ceased 1988, locos used on internal tracks only until 1992.

APPENDIX

Engine No./name	Type	Cyl.	Builder	Works No. & date	Dates on site

Ductile Steels Ltd, Wednesfield

| | 4wDM | | RH | 349039/1953 | 1965-1981 |

Rail traffic ceased around July 1981.

Willenhall Furnace Co. Ltd, Sandbeds, Willenhall

| | 0-6-0 | IC | SB | 538/1848 | |
| Rebuilt to | 0-6-0ST | IC | Crewe | /1860 | 1877-1882 |

Rail traffic ceased 1882.

Birchills Furnaces Ltd, Green Lane Furnaces, Walsall

	0-4-0ST	OC			1907-?
2	0-4-0ST	OC	HL	2728/1907	1907-c.1932
3	0-4-0ST	OC	HL	2739/1908	1908-c.1938

Although the furnaces closed around 1932, the last locomotive remained in its shed for around another six years.

British Electricity Authority (later Central Electricity Authority, then Central Electricity Generating Board), Birchills power station, Walsall

(No. 1) WA No. 2	4wDM		RH	262997/1949	1949-c.7/1982
No. 2	4wDM		RH	275886/1949	1949-c.11/1977
	0-4-0ST	OC	P	1893/1936	7/1951-c.1/1958
3087	0-6-0DE		Derby	/1954	24/10/1973-5/1983

Rail traffic ceased 1980. Peckett 1893 survives as a static exhibit at GWR Museum, Coleford, Gloucestershire.

From Aldridge to Brownhills

Walsall Wood Colliery Co. Ltd, (later National Coal Board), Walsall Wood

Countess of Essex	0-4-0ST	OC	BP	1148/1872	c.1881-c.1894
Cannock Wood	0-6-0ST	IC	Lill	/1870	1882-?
Pelsall	0-6-0T		JS	/c.1865	c.1893-c.1918
Victor	0-6-0T		JS	/c1865	c.1905-c.1920
5 Lord Kitchener	0-6-0ST	IC	K	5158/1915	1915-1951; c.11/1951-c2./1959; 4/1963-4/1965
6 Lord French	0-6-0ST	IC	K	5171/1916	1916-1948
Nuttall	0-6-0ST	OC	HE	1685/1931	7/1948-c.6/1950; 8/1955-8/1956
No. 3 Hanbury	0-6-0ST	IC	P	567/1894	7/1949-c.1953
Aynho	0-6-0ST	IC	MW	1722/1909	c.4/1950-1951
Griffin	0-6-0ST	IC	K	5036/1913	1953-c.8/1955; 3/1956-3/1962
Tony	0-6-0ST	OC	HL	3460/1921	2/1959-5/1965
	0-4-0ST	OC	AB	2247/1948	5/1964-9/1964; 3/1965-5/1965

Colliery closed October 1964, rail traffic ceased after stocks cleared.

The British Steel Corporation works at Wolverhampton (formerly the Osier Bed Iron Works) was latterly used for steel profiling and finishing. It relied on two locomotives, one of which is seen here in April 1979 at the works with the Walsall line in the background. This is Yorkshire Engine Co. 0-4-0DE *Stanton No. 45* (Works No. 2623 of 1956). *K. Lane Collection*

Former BR 0-6-0 diesel shunter No. 3087, sold to the CEGB and repainted into an overall startling orange, performs its duties at Birchills power station around 1968, as children play in the derelict area below the line. *R. Selvey Collection*

BR 350 hp 0-6-0DE No. 3087 was purchased by the Central Electricity Generating Board from BR, arriving on 24th October, 1973 from Springs Branch shed, Wigan. The CEGB repainted it in a striking orange livery, with yellow coupling rods, wasp diagonal stripes on each end, but retained the red buffer beams. Here it seen going about its normal duties of shunting internal user wagons at Birchills power station on 11th April, 1979. *R. Selvey*

The CEGB employed two identical Ruston Hornsby 4-wheel diesel-mechanical type '88DS' locomotives at Birchills power station. Both were supplied new by the manufacturers in 1949. They appear to have spent the later years involved in moving the boiler ash waste to the tip, as in this view, taken around 1969. Unfortunately, it is not known which of the two locomotives is pictured here. *R. Selvey*

Kitson 0-6-0ST *Griffin* (5036/1913) posed at Walsall Wood Colliery on 22nd March, 1958. This engine was transferred to this colliery in 1953 and worked until scrapped on site in March 1962.
Industrial Railway Society/K.J. Cooper Collection

Three Kitson 0-6-0STs were used at Walsall Wood Colliery over the years, two of them being supplied new by the makers, including this one, No. 5 *Lord Kitchener* (5158/1915). It is seen here in snowy conditions at an unknown date. It was eventually cut up at the colliery in April 1965.
Kidderminster Railway Museum/E. Bennett Collection

APPENDIX 167

This chunky Hawthorn, Leslie 0-6-0ST *Tony* (3460/1921) was employed at Walsall Wood Colliery from February 1959 and is seen here in March 1965 having been withdrawn from service. It was scrapped just two months later. *Allan C. Baker*

Engine No./name	Type	Cyl.	Builder	Works No. & date	Dates on site
Coppice Colliery Co. Ltd., Coppice No. 6 and No. 8 Pits, Wilkin, Brownhills					
(*Hanbury*) *Fair Lady*	0-4-2ST	IC	BP	1915/1879	1879-c.1893

Colliery closed c.1893.

Engine No./name	Type	Cyl.	Builder	Works No. & date	Dates on site
Coppice Colliery Co. Ltd., (later National Coal Board), Heath Hayes					
Hanbury	0-6-0ST	IC	P	567/1894	1894-7/1949; c.6/1954-c.1/1959; c.1/1961-2/5/1963
Fair Lady	0-4-2ST	IC	BP	1915/1879	c.1893-1926
2 Thomas	0-6-0T	IC	K	5358/1921	2/1926-c.1953; c.4/1955-13/7/1963
McClean	0-4-2ST	IC	BP	28/1856	c.3/1948-c11/1949
Foggo	0-4-2ST	IC	Chasetown	/1946	c3./1948-c.11/1949; c.3/1954-c.6/1954
Conduit No. 4	0-6-0ST	IC	MW	1326/1891	10/1949-5/1950; 10/1950-c.1951
Nuttall	0-6-0ST	OC	HE	1685/1931	c.6/1950-8/1955
	0-4-0ST	OC	AB	2247/1948	c.5/1959-c.1963; 18/4/1963-10/1963
The Colonel	0-6-0ST	IC	HC	1073/1914	11/7/1963-17/10/1963

Locomotives operated by running powers over BR Five Ways Branch and CCWR to MR sidings at MR Cannock Chase. Rail traffic ceased 27th September, 1963.

Appendix Two

Local trip workings

June 1959 until further notice

Duty No. 328 class '7' freight engine (LNWR 0-8-0) Saturdays excepted
Bescot Shed	8.55 am light engine
Walsall Midland Yard	9.03-9.20 am
return to Bescot Yard	9.33-11.53 am
Walsall Midland Yard	12.04-12.45 pm
Walsall (B. Place)	12.50-1.22 pm
Ryecroft Junction	1.26 pm detaches Willenhall-Wednesfield traffic and attaches Wolverhampton traffic off No. 69
Walsall Midland Yard	2.25-2.45 pm
Birchills Power Sidings	3.01-3.11 pm
Willenhall (Stafford Street)	3.22-3.43 pm
Wednesfield	3.50-4.20 pm
Wolverhampton Midland	4.30-7.00 pm
Wolverhampton LNW	7.15-7.30 pm
Wolverhampton Midland	7.37-8.30 pm
Willenhall (Stafford Street)	8.40-8.50 pm
Aldridge Junction	9.11-9.25 pm
Water Orton	9.54 pm-1.00am

Duty No. 331 class '7' freight engine (LNWR 0-8-0) weekdays
Bescot Shed	4.37 am light engine
Bescot Top Yard	4.57 am
Aldridge Junction	5.24-5.58 am
Washwood Heath	6.55-8.40 am MO/6.58-7.45 am MX
Water Orton	8.00 am MX/9.00 am MO light engine - 9.30 am
Willenhall (Stafford Street)	10.24-10.50 am detaches Willenhall-Wednesfield traffic and attaches Wolverhampton traffic off No. 69
Wolverhampton Midland	11.05-11.30am

	Saturdays only	*Saturdays excepted*
Wednesfield		11.38 am-1.10 pm
Willenhall (Stafford Street)		1.15-1.45 pm
Wye Foundry		1.50-2.05 pm
Short Heath		2.10-3.10 pm
Walsall Midland		3.43-4.02 pm
Bescot Shed	11.52 am light engine	4.10 pm light engine

Duty No. 331 class '7' freight engine (LNWR 0-8-0) weekdays

Bescot Shed	8.43 am light engine
Bescot Old Yard	8.43 am assist No. 69 to Birchills Power Sidings
Birchills Power Sidings	9.55-10.30 am
Ryecroft Junction	10.45-11.00 am
Harrison's Sidings	11.20 am-12.10 pm
Ryecroft Junction	12.35-12.51 pm
Birchills Power Sidings	1.05-1.35 pm

	Saturdays only	Saturdays excepted
Aldridge Junction	2.20-2.50 pm light engine	2.20-2.25 pm light engine
Water Orton	3.15-4.40 pm	
Willenhall (Stafford Street)		4.17-8.00 pm shunt
Wolverhampton Midland		8.09-8.19 pm
Bushbury	5.45-7.05 pm	8.39-9.10 pm
Wednesfield Heath		9.18-9.28 pm
Willenhall (Bilston Street)		9.52-10.02 pm
Darlaston Green Sidings	7.21-7.29 pm	10.09-10.17 pm
Bescot Top Yard	7.39 pm light engine	10.31-11.05 pm
Bescot Old Yard		11.18 pm light engine
Bescot Shed	7.49 pm	11.23 pm

18th June to 9th September 1962

Only those activities occurring on the WWR and WWMJR lines are reproduced here:

Reporting No.	Daily	Class	Description
Duty T38			
9T38		J	9.30 am Water Orton-Willenhall Stafford Street (10.34/10.50) -Wolverhampton Midland 11.05
0Z00	SO	G	11.15 am LE Wolverhampton Midland-Bescot shed 11.37
9T38	SX	J	11.30 am Wolverhampton Midland-Wednesfield (11.38/1.10 pm) -Willenhall Stafford Street (Wye Foundry Siding 1.50/2.05 pm) -Short Heath (2.10/3.00 pm)-Aldridge Junction
0Z00	SX	G	LE 3.40 pm Aldridge Junction-Bescot shed 4.05 pm
Duty T52			
9T52	MX	J	3.30 am Water Orton-Walsall Goods 4.30 am
0Z00	MX	G	4.45 am LE Walsall Down Side-Bescot shed 4.53 am
9T52		J	8.46am Bescot Old Yard - Willenhall Stafford Street (10.11/11.30 SX, 10.11/12.01 SO) - Wednesfield (11.37 SX, 12.08 SO)
0T52		G	EBV 1.00 pm Wednesfield-Wolverhampton Midland 1.05 pm
0T52		G	EBV Wolverhampton Midland-Birchills Power Station 1.40 pm
9T52	SX	J	2.10 pm Birchills Power Station-Bushbury
0T52	SO	G	LE 3.35 pm Birchills Power Station-Bescot shed

Reporting No.	Daily	Class	Description
Duty T54			
0T54	SX	G	3LEs Bescot shed-Walsall Down Side 8.11 am
9T54	SX	J	8.53 am Walsall Down Side-Birchills Siding 9.07 am (assisted by 0T53)
0T54	SX	G	EBV 9.12 am Birchills Siding-Hednesford 9.35 am
9T54		J	1.18 pm Hednesford-Essington Wood Siding (1.48/2.48 SX, 1.48/2.28 SO) Birchills Power Station 3.18 pm SO, 3.40 pm SX
0Z00	SO	G	LE 3.35 pm Birchills Power Station-Bescot shed 3.56pm
7T54	SX	F	4.20 pm Empties Birchills Power Station-Essington Wood Siding 5.08 pm
Duty T56			
7T56		F	10.30 am Empties Birchills Power Station-Anglesea Siding 11.23 am
9T56		J	11.47 am Anglesea Siding-Birchills Power Station 1.05 pm
7T56		F	1.50 pm Empties Birchills Power Station-Aldridge Junction
0Z00	SX	G	LE 2.50 pm Aldridge Junction-Bescot shed
6T56	SO	D	4.40 pm Water Orton-Bescot Down Loop 5.52 pm
Duty T59			
9T59	SO	J	3.40 pm Walsall Down Side-Wolverhampton Midland 4.30 pm
9T59	SO	J	5.15 pm Wolverhampton Midland-Water Orton
9T59	SO	J	7.40 pm Water Orton-Bescot Old Yard 9.44 pm
9T59	SX	J	3.55 pm Walsall Down Side - Willenhall Stafford Street 4.35 pm
7T59	SX	J	7.40 pm Willenhall Stafford Street-Wolverhampton Midland 7.57 pm
7T59	SX	F	8.25 pm Wolverhampton Midland-Aldridge Junction
0Z00	SX	G	LE Aldridge Junction-Bescot shed 9.46 pm

Key
EBV – Engine and brake van
LE – Light engine

Chronology

1865	WWR incorporated (29th June)
1870	Act passed for WWR extension of time (20th June)
1872	WWMJR incorporated (6th August)
	WWR opened to passengers and goods (1st November)
1874	MR decided to build passenger station at Wolverhampton
1875	WWR vested in LNWR (1st July)
	MR started goods services on WWR route
1876	WWR sold by LNWR to MR (1st July)
	Act for construction of Walsall Wood Branch passed (13th July)
	MR took over services on WWR (1st August)
	Wednesfield goods facilities opened
	GWR commenced goods services over WWR
1879	WWMJR opened goods services (19th May)
	WWMJR opened passenger services (1st July)
	Jervis Town station renamed Streetly
1880	Walsall Wood Extension Railway Act passed (6th August)
	Pleck engine shed opened (September)
	Wednesfield Road goods depot, Wolverhampton opened (4th October)
	Walsall goods depot opened
1881	Walsall Wood branch opened for goods traffic (*circa* May)
1882	Walsall Wood Extension to Brownhills opened for goods (1st April)
	Sutton Coldfield station renamed Sutton Coldfield Town (1st May)
	Walsall Wood Extension to Cannock Chase opened for minerals (1st November)
1883	Wolverhampton Canal goods depot opened (spring / summer)
1884	Aldridge to Brownhills opened for passenger traffic (1st July)
1894	Gasworks and sidings opened at Short Heath
	Wilkin Colliery branch closed
1898	Bentley station closed (1st October)
1904	Willenhall Market Place station renamed Willenhall (1st April)
	Sutton Coldfield Town station renamed Sutton Coldfield (1st April)
1909	Traffic sharing agreement between MR and LNWR (1st January)
1910	Heath Town station closed (1st April)
1917	Aldridge to Sutton Park singled (7th January)
	Willenhall to North Walsall singled (4th February)
1921	Aldridge to Sutton Park double track reinstated (20th March)
	Willenhall to North Walsall double track reinstated (8th May)
1924	Brownhills to Cannock Chase singled (13th January)
	Willenhall station renamed Willenhall Stafford Street (2nd June)
	Sutton Coldfield station renamed Sutton Town (2nd June)
1925	Sutton Town station closed (1st January)
	North Walsall station closed (13th July)
	Pleck engine shed closed (2nd September)
1930	Aldridge to Brownhills passenger service withdrawn (31st March)
1931	Wolverhampton to Walsall passenger service withdrawn (5th January)
1936	Penns station renamed Penns (for Walmley) (17th October)
1940	Aldridge to Aldridge Colliery singled (30th June)
	Aldridge Colliery to Walsall Wood singled (7th July)
1949	Birchills Power Station sidings opened (November)
1957	Brownhills to Cannock Chase closed (23rd March)
	World Scout Jamboree at Sutton Park (1st-12th August)
1958	dmus introduced on Walsall to Birmingham (WWMJR) route (17th November)

THE MIDLAND RAILWAY ROUTE FROM WOLVERHAMPTON

1960	Walsall Wood to Brownhills closed (*circa* September)
1962	Walsall goods depot demolished and new depot opened
1964	Heath Town to Ryecroft closed to through traffic (10th August)
	WWR line severed by M6 construction (28th September)
	Aldridge and Sutton Park goods depots closed (7th December)
1965	Walsall to Birmingham passenger services withdrawn on WWMJR route (18th January)
	Penns goods depot closed (1st February)
	Lichfield Road Junction to North Walsall Junction, rail traffic ceased (7th June)
	Aldridge, BICC works to Walsall Wood closed (2nd August)
	Wednesfield goods depot closed (4th October)
	Willenhall goods depot closed (1st November)
	Wednesfield to Bentley closed (1st November)
1966	Wednesfield Road goods depot, Wolverhampton closed by BR
1967	Lichfield Road Junction to North Walsall Junction, line officially closed (1st May)
	Heath Town to Wednesfield mothballed (May)
1968	WWMJR route downgraded to goods line (7th January)
	Park Lane Junction to Water Orton singled (7th January)
1969	Aldridge to BICC works closed (10th February)
	Park Lane Junction to Castle Bromwich Junction singled (3rd August)
	Wolverhampton Canal goods depot demolished, site sold for industrial use
1970	Heath Town to Wednesfield reopened (July)
1978	Rail traffic ceased to Birchills power station (5th December)
1980	Birchills to Ryecroft officially closed (12th May)
1983	Heath Town to Wednesfield closed (November)
1984	Chord to GWR at Wolverhampton taken out of use (October)
	WWMJR route upgraded to passenger status (2nd December)
	Pleck engine shed demolished
1987	Royal Mail sorting centre, Sutton Park - rail services discontinued
1988	Wednesfield Road goods depot, Wolverhampton converted to steel terminal
1994	Wednesfield Road goods depot, Wolverhampton site cleared

English Electric class '37' No. 37008 at Sutton Coldfield with a van train, possibly a Ministry of Defence working from Kineton depot. The date was 17th July, 1990. *R. Monk*

Bibliography and Acknowledgements

Primary documentation has been accessed at the following locations:

The National Archives, Kew – Minutes, selected records and working timetables of the Midland Railway, London & North Western Railway, Wolverhampton & Walsall Railway, Wolverhampton Walsall & Midland Junction Railway and London Midland & Scottish Railway
Staffordshire County Archives, Stafford – Deposited plans, Parliamentary Acts, Ordnance Survey maps
Wolverhampton Archives – Deposited papers, Deposited Plans, Ordnance Survey maps, local maps, *Express & Star*, *Wolverhampton Chronicle*
Birmingham Central Library – Ordnance Survey maps
Stafford Library – *Staffordshire Advertiser*
William Salt Library, Stafford – Parliamentary Acts
Walsall Local History Centre – Ordnance Survey maps, *Walsall Observer & South Staffordshire Chronicle*, *Walsall Chronicle*
Wednesfield Library – local maps
Midland Railway Society Study Centre, Derby – MR working timetables
National Railway Museum – Working timetables
Author's collection – Photographs, public timetables, working timetables and sectional appendices

The following secondary sources of information have been consulted:

Portrait of the Pines Express by S. Austin (Ian Allan, 1998)
Cross City Connections by J. Bassett (Brewin Books, 1990)
A Century of Railways around Birmingham and the West Midlands, Volume 1: 1900-1947 by J. Boynton (Mid England Books, 1997)
Work and Wages by Thomas Brassey (privately published 1874)
The Directory of Railway Stations by R.V.J. Butt (Patrick Stephens, 1995)
A Regional History of the Railways of Great Britain, Volume 7: The West Midlands by R. Christiansen (David & Charles, 1983)
Contractors Locomotives: Part One by D. Cole (Union Publications, 1982)
Contractors Locomotives: Part Three by D. Cole (Union Publications, 1967)
Contractors Locomotives: Part Four by D. Cole (Union Publications, 1970)
Rail Centres: Wolverhampton by Paul Collins (Ian Allan, 1990)
Staffordshire Railways by D.L. Clarke (University of London, Institute of Historical Research, 1967)
Railways of the West Midlands: A Chronology 1808-1954 by C.R. Clinker (SLS, 1954)
The Midland Railway: A Chronology by J. Gough (RCHS, 1989)
Railway Reminiscences by J. Haddock (Walsall Museum & Library Service, 1984)
Walsall's Engine Shed: Railwaymen's Memories, 1877-1968 by J. Haddock (Tempus Publishing, 2006)
The Law Journal for the years 1832-1949 by E.B. Ince (1974)
The Life and Labours of Thomas Brassey by Sir Arthur Helps (1894, reprinted Nonsuch)
Branch Lines of Warwickshire by C.G. Maggs (Alan Sutton Publishing, 1994)
Reports of Cases decided by the English Courts: Volume 6: Great Britain Courts by Nathaniel Cleveland Moak (W. Gould & Sons, 1874)
Railway Reminiscences by George Potter Neale (Reprint EP Publishing, 1974)
The Law Times: Volume 55 by Office of the Law Times (1873)
A Gazetteer of the Railway Contractors and Engineers of Central England 1830-1914 by L. Popplewell (Melledgen Press, 1986)
Brownhills: A Walk into History by G. Reece (Walsall Local History Centre, 1996)
The London & North Western Railway: A History by M.C. Reed (Atlantic Transport Publishing, 1996)

Industrial Locomotives of West Midlands by R.A. Shill
   (Industrial Railway Society, 1992)
Industrial Locomotives of South Staffordshire by R.A. Shill
   (Industrial Railway Society, 1993)
The Industrial Canal: Vol. 2 The Railway Interchange Trade
   by R.A. Shill (Heartlands Press, 1998)
Wednesfield: The Field of Woden by J.L. Smallshire
   (Workers Education Association – Wolverhampton branch)
The History of the Midland Railway by C.E. Stretton (Methuen & Co., 1901)
'Traffic to Birmingham and the Black Country' by K. Turton, *L&NWR Society Journal*,
   Vol.6, No. 4, March 2010
Pregrouping in the West Midlands by P.B. Whitehouse
   (Oxford Publishing Company, 1984)
Railways of the Black Country by N. Williams (Uralia Press, 1985)
Black Country Railways by N. Williams (Alan Sutton Publishing, 1995)
The Midland Railway: Its Rise and Progress - a narrative of modern enterprise
   by F. Smelton Williams (Bemrose, 1878)

Contemporary traffic reports from various issues of *Railway Magazine*, *Trains Illustrated*, *Modern Railways*, *Rail* and *Railway Observer*.
   Websites of the Wolverhampton Local History Society and Willenhall Local History Society.
   This work could not have been completed without the help and enthusiasm of many people, including: Brian Creswell, Simon Dewey, Bill Mayo, Robert Selvey and Tim Shuttleworth. Considerable local input was given willingly and cheerfully by Jack Haddock, who has subsequently and very sadly, since passed away. Finally, I have to acknowledge the help and support of my wife Sandra for giving me inspiration, as well as providing elements of genealogical information.
   Every effort has been made to ensure that photographs used in this work are credited to the appropriate photographer and/or copyright holder. In some cases, the author has not been able to determine the individuals, and apologies are offered to anyone omitted or incorrectly attributed.

Former GWR 'King' class 4-6-0 No. 6024 *King Edward I* working hard on the climb from Walsall towards Aldridge. It is working the 'Cambrian Coast Express' from Shrewsbury to Paddington on 9th June, 2007. The first vehicle behind the locomotive's tender is an auxiliary water carrier. At this point the line runs in a deep cutting in order to pass beneath the Rushall Canal. *Author*

Index

Addison, John, 9, 11, 13, 17, 19, 20, 22, 26, 35, 133, 134, 135

Birchills,
 Furnaces, 61, 66, 163
 Power station, 62, 63, 101, 105, 107, 108, 123, 125, 163
 Sidings, 62, 63, 123
Bradburn, William, 10, 49
Brassey, Thomas, 13
Bushbury, 13, 14, 49, 108

Canals,
 Anson branch, 61, 62
 Bentley, 51, 55
 Birchills branch, 62
 Daw End branch, 67, 136, 141, 143
 Fazeley, 19, 81
 Rushall, 20, 22
 Wyrley & Essington, 7, 27, 33, 34, 41, 43, 49, 55, 62, 136, 143
Collieries,
 Aldridge, 134, 141
 Conduit, 137, 143, 152
 Leighswood, 141
 Walsall Wood, 135, 136, 141, 143, 151, 163
 Wilkin (Coppice Nos. 6 & 8), 133, 137, 143, 161, 167
 Victoria, 141
Contractors,
 Brassey, Ogilvie & Harrison, 11, 13
 Firbank, John, 19, 20, 22, 23
 Garlick, John, 27, 29, 36, 38, 137
 Horsman, P. & Co., 27, 29, 36
 Jeffrey & Pritchard, 21
 Lees Brothers, 36
 Lilley & Son, 22, 30
 Lovatt, Henry, 33, 34, 134, 135, 136

Dixon, Edward, 7, 8

Earle, Ralph Anstruther, 7, 8, 9
Engine sheds,
 Pleck, 25, 37, 109, 113
 Ryecroft, 20, 109, 113
Essington & Ashmore Light Railway, 43

Goods depots,
 Aldridge, 20, 67, 73, 123, 132, 133, 135, 136, 151, 152
 Canal, Wolverhampton, 27, 31, 33, 34, 47
 Mill Street (LNWR), Wolverhampton, 16, 47, 101, 108
 Penns, 81, 96, 113, 123
 Sutton Park, 20, 75, 79, 99, 123
 Walsall (Tasker Street), 25, 34-37, 62, 99, 101
 Wednesfield, 51, 125
 Wednesfield Road, Wolverhampton, 25, 29, 30, 31, 33, 47, 101, 108, 125
 Willenhall, 57, 101, 116
Grand Junction Railway, 6, 9, 16
Great Western Railway, 7, 115, 116

Junctions,
 Castle Bromwich, 84, 105
 Crane Street, 10, 11, 15, 16, 47
 Heath Town, 16, 31, 47, 91, 123, 125, 155
 Lichfield Road, 17, 63, 67, 91, 101, 122
 North Walsall, 17, 63, 67, 101, 108, 123
 Park Lane, 17, 18, 81, 84
 Ryecroft, 7, 10, 17, 21, 67, 91, 123, 125
 Water Orton, 17, 18, 23, 105, 122

Lichfield, Earl of, 7, 8, 15, 61
Line singling, 87, 123

McClean, John Robinson, 21

Osier Bed Iron Works, 34, 47

'Pines Express', 99
Portobello & Wolverhampton Railway, 6

Scout Jamboree, 73, 119, 121, 122
Short Heath gas works, 59
Shrewsbury & Birmingham Railway, 45

Stations,
  Aldridge, 20, 23, 67, 73, 99, 139, 141, 145, 155
  Bentley, 13, 61, 155
  Brownhills, 119, 139, 143, 145, 161
  Heath Town, 13, 49
  North Walsall, 7, 13, 63, 155
  Penns, 20, 23, 79, 81, 99, 121, 155
  Short Heath, 13, 43, 57, 91, 123, 155
  Streetly (Jervis Town), 20, 23, 73, 99, 121, 155
  Sutton Park, 20, 23, 75, 98, 121, 155
  Sutton Town, 20, 23, 79, 119, 155
  Walsall, 17, 25, 122
  Walsall Wood, 135, 137, 139, 141, 145
  Wednesfield, 7, 13, 49, 51, 55, 58, 91, 108, 123, 155
  Wolverhampton High Level, 6, 7, 16, 25, 26, 27, 45, 47, 49
  Wolverhampton Low Level, 25, 45, 47, 119, 122, 125, 155

Stations (*continued*),
  Wolverhampton MR, 25, 26, 27
  Willenhall, 7, 13, 55, 57, 91, 108, 123, 155
  South Staffordshire Railway, 7, 10, 14, 15, 16, 17, 21, 41, 63, 101, 105
  Sutton Park, 17, 18, 63, 75, 96

Traffic sharing, 86, 87

Wednesfield & Wyrley Bank Railway, 41
Wolverhampton & Stour Valley Railway, 6, 45
Wolverhampton & Walsall Bentley branches, 41
Wolverhampton & Walsall Extension Railway, 39, 41

Hunslet 0-6-0ST *Walsall* was built in 1877 (Works No. 188) for use on construction of the WWMJR line. It is shown here in its original cabless condition at an unknown location and date. *Leicester Museums/Industrial Railway Society Collection*